David Thomas is someone I g
to parenting—especially par.
sight, and kindness are unparalleled. *Raising Emotionally Strong Boys* is a book I will keep as an ongoing reference. Thank you for writing this book, David!

Rachel Cruze, #1 *New York Times* bestselling author, host of *The Rachel Cruze Show*

For the past decade, David Thomas has been my go-to boy expert. His newest book, *Raising Emotionally Strong Boys*, unlocked a new level of understanding my four sons. Based on years of counseling boys, David provides insight and practical activities to gently guide you in knowing how to help your son name, regulate, and respond appropriately to his emotions.

Heather MacFadyen, author of *Don't Mom Alone*, host of the *Don't Mom Alone Podcast*

This book is the most impactful, practical, and applicable playbook for raising young men that we have read to date. Our boys will face opponents called pressures, stresses, disappointments, expectations, shame, guilt, anger, sadness, fury, and the fear of not measuring up. Yet with this training manual, we have a plan to champion them as they grow in character with both strength and pliability (tenderness). David, we cannot thank you enough, friend, for coming alongside parents with the truth that these young men can out-score those opponents when they realize the resources surrounding and within them are always greater than what is against them.

Tim and Elisabeth Hasselbeck, college sweethearts, parents of three children; NFL quarterback and ESPN analyst; Emmy Award winner and bestselling author

We've been through deep pain and deeper resilience in our story, but one of our main concerns is how our boys will internalize it all in their own stories. We're so grateful for guides like David—and this book—who help equip us as we humbly parent our kids into the reality that life can be hard but it can also be good, and that what happens to them matters far less than how they respond to it.

Katherine and Jay Wolf, co-authors of *Hope Heals* and *Suffer Strong*

David's book *Wild Things* is one I highly recommend (no, urge) every parent to read. *Raising Emotionally Strong Boys* is no different. Each page leads me into a deeper understanding of my five sons, enables me to meet them where they are, and shows me how to empower them on their path to godly manhood. An absolutely essential read!

Jeannie Cunnion, bestselling author of *Don't Miss Out* and *Mom Set Free*

RAISING
EMOTIONALLY
STRONG BOYS

Other Books by David Thomas

Are My Kids on Track?

Wild Things

RAISING EMOTIONALLY STRONG BOYS

TOOLS YOUR SON CAN BUILD ON FOR LIFE

David Thomas, LMSW

BETHANYHOUSE

a division of Baker Publishing Group
Minneapolis, Minnesota

Published by Bethany House Publishers
11400 Hampshire Avenue South
Minneapolis, Minnesota 55438
www.bethanyhouse.com

Bethany House Publishers is a division of
Baker Publishing Group, Grand Rapids, Michigan

Printed in the United States of America

Library of Congress Cataloging-in-Publication Data
Names: Thomas, David, author.
Title: Raising emotionally strong boys : tools your son can build on for life / David Thomas, LMSW.
Description: Minneapolis, Minnesota : Bethany House Publishers, a division of Baker Publishing Group, [2022]
Identifiers: LCCN 2021058123 | ISBN 9780764239984 (paperback) | ISBN 9780764240713 (casebound) | ISBN 9781493437429 (ebook)
Subjects: LCSH: Child rearing—Religious aspects—Christianity. | Parenting—Religious aspects—Christianity. | Emotions—Religious aspects—Christianity. | Boys—Psychology.
Classification: LCC BV4529 .T458 2022 | DDC 248.8/45—dc23/eng/20220120
LC record available at https://lccn.loc.gov/2021058123

Some names and recognizable details have been changed to protect the privacy of those who have shared their stories for this book.

The information in this book is intended solely as an educational resource, not a tool to be used for medical diagnosis or treatment. The information presented is in no way a substitute for consultation with a personal health care professional. Readers should consult their personal health care professional before adopting any of the suggestions in this book or drawing inferences from the text. The author and publisher specifically disclaim all responsibility for any liability, loss, or risk, personal or otherwise, which is incurred as a consequence, directly or indirectly, of the use of and/or application of any of the contents of this book.

Cover design by Dan Pitts

Baker Publishing Group publications use paper produced from sustainable forestry practices and post-consumer waste whenever possible.

24 25 26 27 28   7

To Lily, Baker, and Witt.
Being your dad has been my greatest joy in this life.

Contents

Foreword by Sissy Goff   11

1. **Traps and Tricks** *Getting emotionally stuck is common for boys. Learn what traps them and how to help them find new plays or "trick shots" to get unstuck.*   15

2. **Foundation and Definition** *Learning regulation skills and building emotional muscles is foundational work. Defining our role in this work as parents is equally important.*   26

3. **Backward and Forward** *Helping boys develop an interior life and strong psychological immune system is key. Learn how to help boys move out of the blame-to-shame swing and into healthy ownership.*   43

4. **Anxiety and Depression** *Understand the unique ways anxiety and depression present in boys and adolescent males. Learn practical skills to help boys navigate fear, sadness, and anger.*   61

5. Moms and Dads *Consider the unique roles each parent plays in a boy's growth and development. Identify the ingredients he needs unique to your gender.* 83

6. Friends and Allies *Develop a better understanding of what upside-down kingdom living looks like in a boy's life and friendships. Identify three different layers of relationships.* 106

7. Models and Mentors *Define* wisdom *and identify the voices that impact your life for good as a parent and those in the life of your son.* 121

8. Upward and Outward *Explore what upward and outward living means and how it contradicts the phrase "man up!" Practice exercises that create concrete upward and outward experiences for boys.* 135

9. Habits and Practices *Help boys build a framework for physical, emotional, relational, and spiritual health. Discover an easy blueprint for building habits and practices.* 150

Conclusion: Moving Forward   173
Acknowledgments   185
Notes   188

Foreword

Boys are bewildering creatures. They're adorable, hilarious, wild, and completely puzzling. It's why I have watched literally thousands of parents—moms, in particular—sit transfixed, listening to and learning from my friend David Thomas. Yes, at first they're transfixed. And then I can see deep, hope-filled relief flood over them. *My son is normal.*

It is truly life-changing for every mom and every grown-up who loves a boy to hear David—who has been counseling boys and their families for almost three decades—say that their little (or big) guy is active and aggressive and curious because he's supposed to be. That, indeed, he *does* act before thinking. That it's all part of how God designed his brain to develop. That there are ways we can interact with him that speak specifically to that design. And that might even help him listen, too.

I have had the honor of working alongside David since 1997. We have practically grown up together in this amazing yellow house called Daystar, where we both have the great privilege of counseling kids and families. (We both started when we were six . . . just kidding; we were in our early twenties.) Since that time, we have spoken together in front of thousands of parents all over the world. We used to joke that he was the Donny to my Marie, until parents in our audiences were too young to know who Donny and Marie are. We've been doing this that long. If you're one of those post–Donny and Marie parents, suffice it to say that we've been great friends who are like brother and sister for perhaps longer than you've been alive. Which means I have had a front-row seat to watch this man deeply impact not just boys of all ages, but their parents and grandparents, as well. And now I get to listen to and learn from him in a whole new way.

As this book is coming out, I have a three-year-old nephew and another little guy on the way in just a few months. I come from a girl family, and I, obviously, am a girl. Just like every mom at our events, I am transfixed hearing David talk about boys. I am in awe, not just at how God designed boys in a way that is profoundly different from how he designed girls, but also at the way David speaks directly about and to the heart of boys.

I also love that, when David was asked about writing a book on anxiety for boys after my book, *Raising Worry-Free Girls*, was released, he said no. Or at least, no to a book that's just about anxiety. Girls are twice as likely to struggle with anxiety as boys are. David knows boys and where they're struggling. He sits with them every day in our counseling office. He knows boys who do suffer from anxiety, but maybe even more struggle with self-regulation, with a surplus of energy and sometimes anger, with difficulty listening, and with a tendency to go outward with their emotions rather than inward. And the boys who do suffer from anxiety often look like they're struggling with something entirely different . . . which is why we need David. David wanted to address where boys are, where specifically they tend to struggle, and what we can do to help.

Bring on this book—for me and for the thousands of parents who get to lean in and learn from the wisdom of David Thomas. I can't wait to help raise emotionally strong boys. And I'm grateful to have an emotionally strong and wise friend to lead the way, someone who has been in the trenches doing so day in and day out for almost thirty years. So grab your highlighter and a cup of coffee, and get ready to learn and laugh about these wonderful, bewildering creatures from a man who I believe is truly the leading expert on raising emotionally strong boys.

Sissy Goff, MEd, LPC-MHSP

Traps and Tricks

grew up in the seventies, and from 1977 to 1982, *The Incredible Hulk* television series ran on CBS. You'd find me glued to the TV each week, awaiting the adventures of Dr. David Banner, a brilliant scientist whose laboratory experiment goes terribly awry. From that moment forward, whenever he is under extreme stress, he undergoes a massive change and morphs into the Incredible Hulk—a tall, muscular, bright-green monster. After destroying whatever threatens Dr. Banner, he morphs back to normal human form, left with his broken memory, tattered clothing, and evidence of destruction. These transformations are quite troubling for Dr. Banner, and he begins a long journey of trying to reverse his condition.

Decades later, I have taken my own sons to the theater to watch the many reimagined versions of this classic story. Each time I watch an interpretation, I'm struck by how it mirrors the work I do as a therapist who counsels boys. I think many boys relate to the Incredible Hulk because they understand the tension of wanting to do good in the world while battling a monster inside. They know the impact of stress and what it's like when it comes out sideways. They understand emotion evolving into a transformation with an undesired outcome.

I've even had parents describe their sons as being like the Hulk. They report sending one guy to school and ending up with a monster at bedtime; these boys regulate with teachers and coaches, and then come unhinged at home with their parents. Recently a mom shared that reminding her son he had five minutes of screen time left resulted in his yelling, throwing the remote, and sobbing uncontrollably on the floor. She laughingly said, "He didn't turn green, but I kept waiting for it to happen."

When we get angry, our nervous system goes into higher states of arousal. We experience sensations in the body from increased heart rate, dilated pupils, adrenaline release, increased respiration, skin perspiration, and blood flow moving to the larger muscles. Sounds a bit like turning into the Hulk, doesn't it?

The Three Rs

Our job is to help boys learn to recognize stress as it registers inside them. We want to train them to observe and pay attention to the body sensations they are experiencing. As important as it is to *recognize* what's happening, boys need instruction in how to *regulate* in these moments. If they struggle to do one or both of those vital tasks, they may have a "Hulk moment" and then need to do some *repair*.

Despite the body's sounding alarms and sending signals, boys often ignore the signs and push forward until they find themselves in tattered clothes and full of regret. I've talked with thousands of boys over the decades who've described what it feels like on the other side of a Hulk moment. Boys share stories of yelling at their mom, shoving a younger sibling, or breaking an object in their home. I've heard adolescent boys describe unloading on a girlfriend, getting a technical foul in a game, or punching a hole in drywall.

The stories often involve blaming others for their mistakes, struggling to take ownership, and swimming in shame and regret. The image of Dr. Banner walking the streets teary-eyed and wondering what just happened comes to mind.

When I track through these stories, boys can often trace the events and identify where they got a signal they ignored or coaching from a parent they bypassed. They might even remember being told they were about to make things worse for themselves, and yet somehow the Hulk emerged.

Teaching the three Rs is something I've believed in for as long as I've been practicing as a therapist. It's the kind of work I believe creates good growth. It's not easy, and boys have a strong tendency to fall back into emotionally lazy responses. After all, it's not that difficult to melt down like a toddler or to lose your mind like a teenager. Regulation is work. It's effortful. But it yields good growth.

Learning to pay attention to the sirens and signals takes reflection, insight, and awareness. It's much easier to ignore the signs and keep your foot on the gas. However, it isn't safer to do so. Equally so, repairing a relationship is work. It requires a posture of humility and civility, and it's much easier to swing between blame and shame. Blame is nothing more than discharged pain. Shame is self-contempt. Neither is a satisfying state of being. The work of relationship, though, is deeply satisfying.

> *Recognize*—notice how your body signals an emotional response
>
> *Regulate*—employ calming strategies when the nervous system goes into higher states of arousal
>
> *Repair*—take ownership and do any needed relational work

Understanding and practicing the three Rs may be the most important coaching we do with the boys in our care. These are the benchmarks of raising emotionally strong boys. As simple as they sound and as necessary as they are to his emotional and relational health, we are somehow missing the mark.

Traps

Stuck. I've used this word in my office for decades. I think getting stuck is part of the human condition. We're all vulnerable to getting stuck in life—physically, emotionally, relationally, spiritually. Sometimes we get ourselves unstuck, and sometimes we need help to do that.

I have a giant Yeti water bottle in my office that serves as a reminder to me to drink eight glasses of water each day. I can get busy and forget to stay hydrated. Some days I fill the Yeti up repeatedly and hydrate like an athlete in training. Other days, I get stuck and forget to drink and refill, ending up with a headache around three in the afternoon, wondering what happened.

I grew up running and swimming competitively. I carried those passions into my adult life, and I've competed in everything from 5Ks to marathons. I've gone for long seasons training like I was headed to the Olympics, and other seasons like I'd never owned a pair of running shoes. I've been stuck in exercising, eating well, praying, friendships, marriage, parenting, vocation, and about every other aspect of life. I've been able to jump-start myself in certain seasons, and in other seasons I've needed help—a coach, a counselor, a friend, a pastor, or my spouse.

Getting stuck is a human condition. Men and women, boys and girls, any one of us can get stuck in any moment, and in any space—physically, emotionally, relationally, spiritually. The difference I've observed in my work is that women are more likely to reach out for help when they get stuck. There are certainly exceptions to this rule. I know women who struggle to ask for help and men who are great at doing so. But generally speaking, males struggle more in this space, and I strongly believe it's connected to our definition of masculinity. A definition many have worked to retire for some time now. For years, we've been working to expand the definition of masculinity, and countless individuals have pushed against the cultural messages we are sending boys about what it means to be a man in this world.

I hope this book can add a brick to the building of something new. I don't believe the traditional definition of masculinity includes tenderness. The longer I study the person of Jesus, the character of Christ, the more I come back to how his strength was founded in tenderness, compassion, mercy, and love. They were the pillars of his humanity.

A foundational part of raising emotionally strong boys includes anchoring them to a clear understanding of the character of Christ and seeing the strength of sacrifice. If we hope to raise boys with relational strength, we need to see a man who walked intimately with a few close friends. As we evaluate his interaction and conversations with the disciples, his closest companions, we see intimacy and vulnerability. We see a man who celebrated and elevated women. We see a man who was constantly challenged and questioned throughout his ministry and somehow never went off the rails.

> Jesus's strength was founded in tenderness, compassion, mercy, and love.

Jesus, in his humanity, was full of emotions. He wept with his dear friend Mary at the loss of her brother, Lazarus (John 11). When he encountered the tax collectors using the temple for purposes never imagined, he felt anger (Matthew 21). In the garden, as he was wrestling with his impending death, and his closest friends fell asleep after he'd asked them to stay awake with him, we're told he felt fear (Matthew 26).

Boys will experience every one of those emotions—sadness, anger, fear. Our job is to help them identify what they feel and what to do with those emotions. Recognize, regulate, and if necessary, repair.

Trick Shots

For years, I've talked with boys about their fascination with Dude Perfect. If you aren't familiar, it's a group of former college roommates, a sports and comedy group, who have one of the most-subscribed sports channels on YouTube. These guys created a whole new genre in sports and trick shots. I love building on this fascination by talking with boys about a different kind of trick shot. If stress is part of the game of life, let's develop some plays to move through it. If the typical guy struggles with off-loading stress, what could it look like to develop some trick shots in this space? I routinely have boys leave my office with a list of things that trigger stress for them and ways to manage it.

We talk about the ultimate trick shots of breathing and movement. Learning to do some deep breathing can be a game changer for any young man working with anger, stress, fear, or anxiety. Boys have a lot of physicality to their emotions. Having a physical release is foundational to navigating strong emotions. I have boys create a Top Five List on a note card or device with the majority of the five strategies involving movement to honor this unique way God hardwired males.

The list might include running laps or shooting hoops, pull-ups or push-ups, using a boxing bag or yoga mat, jumping on a trampoline or riding a bike, lunges or jumping jacks, screaming into a pillow or punching it, walking the dog or climbing a tree, and the list goes on and on. I once worked with a twelve-year-old boy who off-loaded stress by riding a unicycle in his driveway, and a sixteen-year-old who washed and waxed his car. I'm open to anything that does involve movement and doesn't involve a screen. Boys often attempt to sell me on how video games or scrolling through social media helps them relieve stress. I'm quick to remind them that screens are an escape, not a coping strategy.

Screens are an escape, not a coping strategy.

As we'll discuss more throughout this book, boys are instinctively skilled in numbing out, and we always want to be training them toward healthy coping. Technology has become one of the most addictive and accessible forms of numbing out for boys of all ages. I'm not opposed to boys having screen time with good limits, but not for the purposes we're discussing. The only exceptions I've made in this space would be for boys who are highly skilled in practicing healthy habits and who choose to add in some breathing and mindfulness apps. This can be a great resource and tool, but apps won't be a starting point.

A Different Direction

Years ago, I came across a viral video of a little boy in the driveway with his younger sister.[1] He looked to be about five years old. She might have been three. He was teaching her to shoot a basketball into a small Fisher-Price goal.

He moved aside to cheer her on. In her first attempt, she not only missed the shot, but the ball bounced back and hit her in the face. She burst into tears and her brother ran to her and hugged her immediately. "It's okay. You're strong," he said, and then he put his hands on both sides of her face and asked, "Do you want me to carry you?"

She agreed to that plan.

He then ran to get the ball, handed it back to her and said, "Now I'm going to carry you." He picked up his little sister to make the shot easier, and she gave it another try. This time she experienced success as her father and her brother cheered.

I watched the video a dozen times, smiling and weeping at the sight of this supportive big brother. I found myself wondering many things about him.

I wondered what his parents are like, and how they nurtured this kind of empathy and compassion.

I wondered how his little sister will be shaped by having a brother who cheers her on throughout life.

I wondered if he'll stop being supportive at some point and become more hardened by the world. I wondered why this instinctive response in boys seems to go away as they travel through development.

A decade ago, I coauthored a bestselling book on boys called *Wild Things: The Art of Nurturing Boys*. I defined five stages of development in the first third of the book. This young boy in the video looked to be in the Lover stage. If I could freeze a boy in one stage of his development, I'd freeze him in the Lover stage. I describe young men here as tender and obedient, relational and compassionate. Obviously he can't stay in that stage forever. He can't stay more than a few years before it's time to move into the complicated stages of pre-, mid-, and late adolescence. He then moves into the vulnerable space of young adulthood. Each stage leading him further away from boyhood and into manhood. What if the journey could look different?

Boys and men lead some of the scariest statistics out there. Research reminds us that males have more difficulty identifying how they feel, resist taking action when they are struggling, are more reluctant to opening up, and engage in more risk-taking behaviors. Unless we create a different direction, the statistics will only get worse. During the global pandemic of 2020, rates of anxiety, depression, and suicide climbed at an unprecedented pace. Existing problems became significantly worse. It served as a harsh reminder that we aren't doing enough to equip the kids we love to navigate the hard seasons of life.

I'm deeply encouraged by the efforts of many to redefine strength and bravery for the girls we love. I'm hopeful we can do the same for boys. What would it look like to raise a generation of boys who see vulnerability as a strength? What would it be like to raise a generation of young men who see prioritizing their mental health as wisdom?

Emotionally strong males are

Resourceful—*having the ability to name and navigate emotions*

Aware—*having a rich interior world, including strengths and weaknesses*

Resilient—*having the capacity to cope and feel competent*

Empathetic—*having an ability to understand and share the feelings of another*

How could we push against the images boys see and offer a new definition of masculinity? How could we anchor boys more strongly to the character of Christ and the qualities of tenderness, compassion, mercy, and love? I believe it's possible. It's much like what we discussed earlier—it will be hard work, but it leads to good growth. I believe it's not only possible, but it's what boys deserve from the grown-ups who love them.

Let's take that journey together.

INTENTIONAL PRACTICES

1. **The Hulk.** Find a cartoon or live movie version of the Hulk you could watch (in full or in part) with a boy you love that illustrates both the transformation and the regret. Talk about the tension between the desire to do good and the capacity for destruction in an age-appropriate way to set the stage for more understanding.

2. **Define the three Rs.** Discuss and define each one. Talk about the goal of becoming skilled in only needing the first two most of the time and about using the third *R* when we make mistakes.

3. **An example.** Invite boys to identify males in their lives (grandparents, teachers, coaches, pastors, and friends) who seem to have strong skills in the three *R*s.

4. **Scripture.** Read John 11:17–35, Matthew 21:12–13, and Matthew 26:36–46 as reminders of how Jesus felt different feelings throughout his time on earth. Read Luke 19:41–48, a back-to-back account of Jesus weeping out of his love for Jerusalem in approaching the city and then right after his cleansing of the temple. Talk about when different emotions happen in close proximity to one another.

5. **Emotionally strong.** Come up with your own definition of what it means to be emotionally strong. Identify characters in books, films, and moments in history in whom you've seen evidence of this kind of strength.

Foundation and Definition

My grandfather came home from World War II and was a builder the rest of his working life. He had six children. His firstborn was a son. This boy had a weak heart and lived only a few hours. My grandparents went on to have five daughters. Each of their daughters had only daughters themselves, except for my mom. I was the only grandson. My grandfather hoped I would someday become a builder, and he could pass on what he had built to me.

When I was in high school, I went to work for my grandfather. I spent one summer building a house alongside my grandfather and his crew of men. We poured a foundation, framed the house, and built walls, and I watched it go from a piece of land to a home where the same family still lives to this day.

I remember watching the foundation being poured. My grandfather smiled throughout the process. It must have been like the smell of freshly sharpened pencils on the first day of elementary school for a teacher, or laying down the first track for a musician recording a new record. The sight, smell, and sound of a new beginning.

I remember him saying the foundation looks unimpressive, but it's potentially the most important step in the build. If a beautiful home is built on a weak foundation, it won't be beautiful for long.

I live in a home that was built in the 1930s in a historical part of our city. Our house is fast approaching its one-hundredth birthday. The home is certainly showing signs of its age, but the day we bought it our Realtor said, "The bones are good."

Similarly, relationships built on a solid foundation can withstand the storms of life. Couples who invest in their relationship with reading, premarital counseling, date nights, active listening, marital work, and other resources can lay a solid foundation they build on through parenting.

The same is true for us as individuals and will be true for our children. When we lay a solid foundation—emotionally, relationally, and spiritually—we have the capacity to weather the storms of life differently.

Jesus said,

"Therefore everyone who hears these words of mine and puts them into practice is like a wise man who built his house on the rock. The rain came down, the streams rose, and the winds blew and beat against that house; yet it did not fall, because it had its foundation on the rock. But everyone who hears these words of mine and does not put them into practice is like a foolish man who built his house on sand.

The rain came down, the streams rose, and the winds blew and beat against that house, and it fell with a great crash."

Matthew 7:24–27

We will talk more in later chapters about what it means to put these words into practice, but for now let's look at the ingredients of an emotional foundation for boys.

The Milestones

In my book *Are My Kids on Track? The 12 Emotional, Social, and Spiritual Milestones Your Child Needs to Reach*, I define four emotional milestones for boys and discuss the stumbling blocks and building blocks to getting there.

The first is the milestone of *vocabulary*. This milestone is all about developing emotional literacy, or the ability to identify, understand, and respond to emotions in oneself and others in a healthy way. I'd love every home and classroom across the globe to have a feelings chart hanging somewhere. This concept is no different from having the letters of the alphabet hanging in classrooms across the world. We understand that letters form words and words form sentences, and these are the foundational building blocks of reading. When kids can see the letters, it strengthens the cognitive connection. The same is true if they can see expressions, make connections with the emotions, and learn to identify those feelings inside of themselves.

Developing toward this milestone feels as important as ever. In this day and age, kids and teens are using bigger and bigger words to articulate their experience—words that aren't necessarily accurate to their experience. I rarely hear teens say, "I feel sad"; they say, "I feel depressed." They don't say, "I feel worried"; they say, "I have anxiety." Some do; many do not. In the past, if kids felt really angry with their parents and wanted to get their attention, they might say, "I'm running away from home!" I almost never hear a parent report a kid saying that anymore. Kids now say, "I'm going to kill myself," or "I should just die."

Many times those declarations are wild cards, covering all sorts of feelings. Boys throw out wild cards often, especially those with an underdeveloped emotional vocabulary. They are trying to cue the grown-ups around them to an emotional storm inside of them, and they say the biggest, scariest thing they know to say.

It feels important to pause here and clearly state that not every boy who makes this kind of declaration is throwing a wild card. Some boys are experiencing true suicidal ideation and need an immediate intervention by professionals. Whether he is suicidal or not, it's a cry for help. He's either needing support in keeping himself safe, or help developing a more accurate way of articulating his experience. Either way, he needs help. Our job is to identify the right kind of support.

In summary, it's never been more important to help boys and adolescent young men develop an emotional vocabulary and name what they feel accurately.

The second emotional milestone is *perspective*. This milestone is learning to accurately categorize the events of life. Learning that a one in life is losing my car keys and a ten is losing a family member. I don't want to go to ten over losing a scrimmage, though many boys can and do.

The milestone of perspective is like the pain scale doctors use. The doctor needs me to *accurately* describe my pain in order to *appropriately* treat my pain. I sit with parents every day who describe boys who haven't developed perspective. They go off the rails over insignificant events.

Kids, more than ever, are swinging to ten for any event in life. They can't scale their experience.

"I had the worst day ever."

"Everyone hates me."

"I should just die."

I want to encourage you to create a perspective scale with your son in a *non-problematic* moment. Don't do this in close proximity to a meltdown. Sit down in a calm, relaxed, rested moment and draw a line across a piece of paper, much like a timeline. Mark off and number one to ten. Have him identify examples of his one to ten events. It's okay to brainstorm with him if he gets roadblocked. Keep in mind that his scaling may look very different from yours. Your job is to help him develop *his* scale, not to adopt yours.

Then use it as a reference point in the harder moments of life to help him accurately categorize his experience. After giving him time to regulate and settle (we will talk more about how to do this throughout the book), ask, "What number do you think that event was?" Or, "What number would you give today?"

It's vital that we are moving boys toward the milestone of perspective throughout their development for all the events they will face in adolescence, in young adulthood, and as adults.

The third emotional milestone is *empathy*. Empathy is a well-researched, foundational ingredient in all healthy interpersonal relationships—spouse to spouse, parent to child, friend to friend, coworker to coworker. It's the ability to understand and share the feelings of another person.

Empathy is a game changer within relationships, and a lack of empathy can tear a relationship apart. Empathy includes active listening and using statements like "What I hear you saying is," or "I wonder if you are needing," or "That sounds really hard."

Empathy is moving outward with emotions. It's the ability to slip into another person's shoes and offer understanding of their emotional experience. However, if I can't read, name, and scale my own emotions, I'll certainly struggle to show up with others in theirs.

The fourth emotional milestone is *resourcefulness*. It's the ability to take the emotion to something constructive. It's the wisdom expressed in Ephesians 4:26: "In your anger do not sin." You're going to feel anger. Just don't hurt yourself or others when you do.

Resourcefulness is one of the places where I see boys getting roadblocked the quickest. It takes work to regulate. It takes work to move the emotion in a healthy direction. Most boys fall back on lazy responses, avoiding the work of resourcefulness. They melt down, scream, hit, or throw things. The work feels hard or sometimes just unfamiliar.

Think about how often boys answer questions with "I don't know."

How do you feel? "I don't know" or "Fine."

Fine is an acronym for Feelings In Need of Expression. Digging in to figure out what I feel is *work*. Saying "I don't know" is easy and lazy. We want to coach boys in the hard work of building emotional muscles. I believe these four milestones are like muscles. For many boys the muscles are simply weak or underdeveloped. But we know weak muscles can get stronger with work. Building emotional muscles is some of the most important, yet most neglected, work in a boy's journey to manhood. The muscles impact his everyday experience as a son, brother, student, athlete, and friend. These muscles will define who he is as a husband, father, friend, and coworker.

The Space

Boys have a lot of *physicality* to their emotions. It's why toddler-aged boys are more prone to biting, hitting, kicking, and screaming. Teenaged boys are more prone to yelling and punching walls or kicking doors. We have to teach them to turn that energy, intensity, and physicality in a constructive direction. When I teach I often show a YouTube video of a toddler filmed by his mother at home. The video opens with the boy rolling around on the floor, having an epic meltdown. The mother keeps the camera on but quietly moves to another room. The crying and yelling quiets, and suddenly there is silence. About that time, the boy moves to the room where his mom is, and as soon as he catches sight of her, he collapses on the floor and starts the meltdown all over again. The mother quietly moves to another room with the camera still recording and suddenly the meltdown stops again. The boy walks to the next room and collapses another time. The cycle repeats itself multiple times, and by this point in my teaching the roomful of parents watching are howling in laughter. Mostly because we all understand the reality of this cycle. It's a pattern we call *anchoring*. It's a boy's way of saying, "If I feel discomfort on the inside, I'd like to tie an anchor around your waist and drag you to the bottom of the ocean with me." It's part of the old saying "Misery loves company."

Unless we teach him something different and coach him consistently, he will always fall back on anchoring. By the time he hits adolescence, he'll be well versed in anchoring. Most boys anchor to their mothers. Many boys who have a history of anchoring to their moms can translate that over to their girlfriends in adolescence.

It's more than appropriate for a boy's mom, or the other females in his life, to be a sounding board, but not a verbal punching bag. We'll talk more about this in chapter 5, "Moms and Dads."

I believe in creating a space—an actual physical space—where a boy can go to release this intensity. Boys twelve and under think concretely. The world is very black-and-white. They don't begin to develop abstract thinking until closer to adolescence. Boys are often slower to develop this than girls. He benefits from concrete experiences. This would involve going to an actual space (a corner of a play room, rec room, mudroom, garage, etc.) and filling this space with tactile experiences like a kick stand, a punching bag, oversized pillows (to hit or scream into), stress balls, a pull-up bar, a mini trampoline, a yoga mat, or an exercise ball (to throw or push against). We are simply brainstorming options that create a release, honoring his need to expend the physicality of the emotion. Some boys are less physical and more artistic. He may prefer a bucket of crayons and paper, other art supplies, or a journal. He might like balloons to blow up, Bubble Wrap to punch and pop, or clay to shape and mold.

When my sons were toddlers, I found an inflatable object with sand in the bottom. I purchased it online and placed it, with some oversized pillows and a bean bag, in the corner of our playroom. We'd walk to that corner together and practice using the objects to release some energy. There was always a feelings chart hanging somewhere. We'd talk about this being a good place to go when we had big feelings inside of us that needed to come out. The objective was to help them get from chaos to calm.

When my sons were emotionally charged and prone to hitting or simply melting down and rolling on the floor like the boy in the video, I'd grab their hands and head to the Space with them. Doing this work *with* them and *alongside* them is co-regulation. Eventually boys go the Space on their own and can do the work or regulation independently. The journey from co-regulation to regulation is similar to the approach I took when teaching my kids to ride a bike. In the beginning, I was always with them, offering support and help for the unfamiliar parts of learning a big new skill. I would hold the handlebars while they did the pedaling, then I would hold their backs to help steady them while they pedaled and steered the bike. Eventually I would run beside them cheering them on, and then stand at a distance to offer support if needed.

When we haven't been on the bike in some time, we can get rusty and need support until we find ourselves back in the rhythm of pedaling and steering.

Also, some kids take to it almost immediately, and others struggle greatly. I know kids who fling their bikes into a ditch when they fall off, yelling, "I'm never getting on that dumb thing again." Some kids have difficulty keeping the bike balanced. Some kids can't get the start of pedaling or the stop of braking. We have to labor longer with some kids and shorter with others. The same will be true with boys and the Space. Remember that practice makes progress.

Most of us grew up being told that practice makes perfect. Let's throw that statement out. I don't think it's true. There are plenty of things in life I've practiced hard at, and not only did I not get perfect at them, I never got all that good at some of them either. But everything I've ever practiced, I got a bit better at over time. We're looking for *progress*, not *perfection*.

We're also remembering this is hard work for many boys. Their tendency will be to fall back on the familiar and instinctive response of anchoring. Our tendency may be to rescue him in these moments. Doing the emotional work for him is the equivalent of doing his homework. He will never get the benefit of learning unless he does the work himself. It's the only way he makes needed connections.

Think for a moment on that analogy. Many boys experience discomfort in doing homework. They become emotionally charged when it's time to sit down, unzip the backpack, and attend to the work. Some boys resist, some whine or throw books when the work gets hard, others melt down in a variety of ways. If we were to do the work for him, it would certainly make the meltdown stop, but he'd have only learned to fall apart rather than push through.

Heading to the Space is like sitting with him for a moment while he regulates and develops a plan for moving forward. Boys are action-oriented creatures. They simply need help activating their innate problem-solving

Boys are action-oriented. They simply need help activating their innate problem-solving abilities.

abilities. Avoid the trap of becoming his resources so he can develop resourcefulness.

The Long Game

I mentioned how our family approached the Space when our boys were toddlers. Let's talk for a moment about how it can develop as boys grow forward. The Space should evolve and change as they do. Encourage boys to keep reimagining it and paying attention to what's helping them.

We moved from the inflatable to a real kick stand I purchased at a used sporting goods store. It looked like those found in martial arts studios. They could punch and kick as often as needed. We added a medicine ball, a mini trampoline, and a bucket of stress balls we made from flour and balloons.

We then moved the Space to the basement of our house and purchased a pull-up bar, a full-size punching bag, and some light weights. It looked more like a workout space as my sons moved into middle school and high school.

As we trained in this direction, it was common for me to come home to the sounds of punching and grunting. Sometimes the punching would stop and I'd hear crying. When I gave that a little time and then checked in, I heard stories of not getting picked for a team, feeling betrayed by a friend, bombing a test, or being frustrated with work. All the normal things that kids face in this world as they travel from elementary school to high school.

Along the way, my sons played countless sports that offered a release. Practices became a place to release stress as well as learn new skills and enjoy friends. My sons fell in love with running. Throughout high school they ran cross-country and track. Running became the Space for both of them. They'd learned to listen to their bodies and pay attention to the signals they were getting when different emotions registered.

There's a great chance running may be that outlet for most of their lives. My job was simply to build a Space for release, usher them toward the Space, be with them in it as they learned its value, and watch them modify it to their needs as they grew.

The actual Space isn't magic. The objects in it aren't magic. The magic is in the experience of going to the Space. The magic is in moving away from anchoring and toward resourcefulness. It takes practice. Years and years of practice.

As he is practicing going to the Space, we are practicing not allowing him to anchor to us. We have to allow the boys we love to struggle. Struggle is good soil for growing resilience and resourcefulness. They can't develop strong emotional muscles unless they use them.

We certainly want to offer empathy and support. We don't want to do the work for him.

Go to the Space when he won't. Many boys are stubborn and will work hard to bait you back into anchoring. See this journey like a tug-of-war. The game of tug-of-war is officially over when one player drops the rope. Even if he is holding on to the rope with tight hands, you can learn to set it down. Sometimes this may feel like the opposite of support. We certainly will

> **Struggle is good soil for growing resilience and resourcefulness.**

only be doing this after many hours of training. Go back to the example of bike riding. No parent would simply hand over a bike without instruction or support and say, "Let me know how it goes." We know we'll be holding the handlebars and the back of the seat in the beginning. We know we'll be running beside them and cheering them on. This is co-regulation. We are helping them regulate until they can do that work themselves.

In summary, you're hearing me say clearly there is *work* involved for you and for him. We can only take the boys we love as far as we've gone ourselves. If regulation is difficult for you, it will be almost impossible for him. Kids learn more from observation than information. He has to see this practiced by the grown-ups he trusts.

He needs to hear you using an expansive emotional vocabulary. He needs to hear you articulate your experience and see that adults have emotions. He needs to hear you identify what helps you work through moments when you are emotionally charged, how your body signals you, and what you do to bring yourself back to a state of calm. But he doesn't just need to hear it; he needs to see it.

He needs to see and hear this to develop a full, expansive, healthy, accurate definition of masculinity.

A New Definition

Historically, boys have been told showing emotion is a sign of weakness. Traditional masculinity is associated with suppressing emotion and self-reliance. What would it look like to raise a generation of boys who saw vulnerability as a strength?

Men lead the statistics for substance abuse, suicide, infidelity, and internet pornography. Men are often skilled in avoiding pain and numbing discomfort. They struggle greatly with asking for help and attending to their health and well-being. What if we raised a generation of boys that saw prioritizing mental health as wisdom?

By nine to ten years of age, boys begin to channel all primary emotions—fear, sadness, disappointment—into anger. We further this culturally by sending messages that it's okay to be angry, but weak to be sad or afraid. Boys are flooded with images of professional athletes blowing up at opponents and coaches screaming at referees. They hear entertainers raging on social media and politicians yelling over one another in debates. In their own homes, they often sit front row to fathers struggling to manage their own emotions. It seems that everywhere they turn, they see a lack of regulation and restraint. They witness men struggling to name their experience and deal with life on life's terms. How could we push against these images and offer a new definition?

As God's image bearers, part of laying a healthy foundation is accurately defining masculinity by looking through the lens of Jesus as a man. His strength was defined by sacrifice, humility, compassion, and love. He had close relationships with a small group of men. He was a champion of women. Scripture tells us Jesus wept in an encounter of loss, felt anger at injustice, and experienced fear in his last hours. Scripture is full of examples of Jesus feeling different things in his humanity. Despite being tempted, challenged, betrayed, mocked, abandoned, abused, and then crucified—the worst of human conditions imaginable—he navigated each of those emotions and experiences with honesty, humility, civility, and strength. His life serves as the ultimate roadmap for how to be a man in this world.

Despite having such clarity about how Jesus lived, we've managed to move so far from his example. But we can move boys back in that direction. I believe it's key to raising emotionally strong boys as they are bombarded with opposing images. It will be countercultural, but the way of Jesus has always involved living in this world and not of it.

Imagine, for a moment, that we began to prioritize emotional health with boys the way we prioritize youth sports or academics in this country. That we began to turn our time and attention in this direction, believing it was of the greatest importance with the longest benefit.

> For we are co-workers in God's service; you are God's field, God's building. By the grace God has given me, I laid a foundation as a wise builder, and someone else is building on it. But each one should build with care. For no one can lay any foundation other than the one already laid, which is Jesus Christ.
>
> 1 Corinthians 3:9–11

The summer I spent building with my grandfather brought great clarity to both of us. As much as he'd hoped to hand over the business to me someday, watching me with a hammer made it evident that my calling would never be in building homes. While I loved working with my grandfather, I felt called to different work. I became a builder of men. I learned how to build *into* people.

I learned this from my father and countless men who have fathered me as well. I learned how to build into people from my mother and the many amazing women I've had the privilege of knowing, sharing life with, and working alongside. I'm still learning how to do this work, and I hope I'm still learning for as long as I'm breathing. This much I know to be true. There is a better, different, healthier, and holistic way to raise the boys in our care. The fact that you're holding this book is evidence you want something different. Let's continue laying a new foundation.

INTENTIONAL PRACTICES

1. **Feelings chart.** Download or purchase a feelings chart to begin helping him develop an emotional vocabulary. Use it often as a point of reference.

2. **Perspective scale.** Create a perspective scale with him at an unproblematic time that you can reference on the other side of emotionally charged moments to help him accurately categorize the events of life.

3. **The Space.** Talk with him about the physicality of his emotions and the importance of releasing that energy. Identify a place in your home that could serve as an outlet for anyone in the family and brainstorm tactile experiences for the Space.

4. **Travel Space.** Purchase a bin for your vehicle that could allow the concept of the Space to go with you anywhere (restaurants, grandparents' house, rides home from school, etc.), and fill it with stress balls, fidget toys, hand weights, journals, or other objects or activities to allow for release away from home.

5. **Define masculinity.** Sit down with him—throughout his development—to define and redefine what it means to be a man. Use media to assess how the world defines masculinity and the Bible to develop an accurate definition.

Backward and Forward

Jake is a sixteen-year-old client whose girlfriend was grounded by her parents. They allowed their daughter to text my client as a courtesy before they took her phone to let him know he'd need to cancel their weekend plans as a result of her grounding.

She apologized to Jake for making a choice that ended up affecting him as well. She knew he'd been making plans for their weekend and would be upset by this news. He fired back a text declaring her parents were making a mistake, and he was furious at their decision.

She told him they'd talk more at school and find another time to be together when the grounding was over. Jake waited approximately thirty seconds and then texted his girlfriend's father. He let the father know he'd made plans for the weekend and asked him to reconsider.

The father responded to Jake, acknowledging his disappointment, imagining the frustration, and hoping they could reschedule once the grounding was lifted.

Jake texted the father again declaring the dad had made a HUGE mistake and would regret the decision.

At this point in our conversation, I asked Jake how much time passed between the dad's response and his text about the huge mistake. "Maybe a minute," he reluctantly answered. We explored what he could have done to collect his thoughts and consider his response. We began discussing how he could salvage the text exchange when Jake confessed it didn't end there.

"You texted again?" I asked.

When Jake confirmed he did, I asked him to pull out his phone and read the text exchange aloud for the purpose of learning. He was hesitant to do so, but could see I wasn't budging. Here's where the conversation went next.

The dad: *Jake, I understand you are frustrated. I can tell you were trying to create a wonderful experience for my daughter on Saturday. I know there will be another time soon when you can enjoy time together. Let me suggest for now that we stop texting while you are clearly feeling a range of emotions. I understand it's easy to say a lot when you're feeling a lot. You're a great boyfriend, and I know this has to be disappointing.*

Jake: *I am a great boyfriend! And I do have a lot to say! I don't want to stop texting because I want you to understand how big a mistake you're making!*

44

The dad: *I'm sure you have a lot to say. I'm convinced now is **not** the right time to say those things. Let's stop while we are ahead. I look forward to seeing you in the near future.*

Jake: *I want to come over to the house and let's talk this out. I need to see her, and I need you to see how wrong this is.*

The dad: *Jake, now isn't a good time for a visit, and it's turning out to be a bad time for you and me to be texting. I'm jumping off and we will talk later.*

Jake: *Why are you doing this? It's no wonder your daughter would rather open up to me than you.*

As Jake read his last text response, I remember thinking, *I'm so glad this father has a teenager he just grounded and knows that sometimes adolescents go off the rails.*

Blame and Shame

I started by asking Jake how he felt in rereading his words. At first, he made an attempt at blaming the father for "why this whole thing happened in the first place."

I invited him to think less about what came first and more about his response. He was up for the challenge and began to tiptoe into making some needed connections. Sadly, this was roadblocked by some self-contempt. "I'm such an idiot. I'm a complete screw-up."

This swing from blame to shame is one that boys make often. They struggle to get to the healthy middle space of taking ownership and rebuilding anything that needs repairing.

Just yesterday I met with a family navigating divorce. The father has had two affairs. The second one was discovered when his oldest son found a photo of his dad kissing another woman. When the truth came out, he said to his son, "I'm sorry you found that," but he never said, "I'm sorry I did that." He, like many boys, was more concerned about getting caught than what he'd done wrong. Unless boys learn to land in the healthy middle ground of ownership, they can stay stuck swinging between blame and shame for a lifetime. If he can't get to ownership, he certainly can't move toward repair.

> Unless a boy learns to take ownership, he can stay stuck swinging between blame and shame.

To help Jake move in that direction, we spent time imagining what the father was experiencing in asking Jake to postpone the conversation until he was in a better head space and Jake's plowing right through his request. We unpacked Jake's accusations, declarations, and assumptions. I asked him to brainstorm what he could have done besides texting when he felt alarms going off inside of him.

Time and Space

Jake was willing to take this journey with me. It's important to note that he'd had some time between the incident and our conversation. *Time and space* can change the game for all of us. We often try to rush the connections or force the conversation before boys are ready. Any time a parent or a child is in an emotionally charged space, it's a bad time to do much talking.

Furthermore, it's not a good time for discipline. Discipline is all about learning. We want kids to make the needed connections that allow for new behaviors next time. If they aren't regulated, they can't make the connections. If we aren't regulated, we're likely to shame, over-discipline, yell, or lecture. Recognize. Regulate. Repair.

What Jake needed was the opportunity to think backward and forward. He needed to reflect on what he'd done to inform what he'd do next.

He didn't need me to fill in the blanks for him, only to be a sounding board as he worked his way through what had happened and how this could inform the next time he got news that wasn't to his liking.

Part of thinking forward involved making decisions on how he wanted to talk with his girlfriend about trust he'd broken with her parents. Thinking forward involved a plan of action for repairing damage he'd done with her father.

Thinking forward involved locking in strategies to combat the impulsivity that every adolescent boy is vulnerable to experiencing in any given moment.

Thinking forward included finding a weekend when he could execute the plans he'd had in place for the original date.

Boys who can't look backward and think forward are left with the emotion of the present. When boys let emotions drive the car, without factoring in thinking, the outcome can be dangerous.

Technology has allowed boys to do many things, one of those being communicating immediately. He doesn't have to wait to call, text, post, tweet, or send. I would argue that technology has trained all of us against regulation and not toward it.

> Fools find no pleasure in understanding
> but delight in airing their own opinions. . . .
> To answer before listening—
> that is folly and shame.
>
> Proverbs 18:2, 13

We have to train ourselves not to react in real time, because we certainly have the tools to do so. Furthermore, we have the instincts to do so. Scientists from the University of Bristol studied content posted to Twitter over twenty-four-hour periods for four years. An analysis of 800 million tweets found analytical thinking didn't begin to peak until *after* six in the morning, with a more impulsive, emotional mode of engagement peaking between three and four in the morning.[1] This information serves as one more reason why teenagers benefit from charging their phones overnight in a central location and not their bedroom. I've had countless parents report finding destructive texting, posting, and internet use in the middle of the night.

Regardless of time of day, any one of us is more vulnerable to tweetstorm behavior when we post, text, tweet, or fire back a response in an emotionally charged moment. I'd argue that regulation is some of the most important emotional work we can do as adults to position ourselves to model and teach this to the kids we love. We can only take the kids we love as far as we've gone ourselves. If regulation is a hurdle for you as a parent, that's the place to begin.

It's difficult for kids to learn to be more responsive than reactive when they can't see it in the adults they trust the most in this world.

Write It Down

Years ago I counseled another young man who was equally reactive by nature. He would blurt out answers in class, interrupt friends when they were talking, correct his siblings, and even sometimes challenge his coaches.

Things came to a head when his parents discovered he'd texted his girlfriend stating his love for her, how he didn't want to live without her, and how he couldn't go on if they ever broke up. This exchange was birthed out of a conflict he and his girlfriend had experienced that left her feeling vulnerable, responsible, and scared for his safety. Her parents reached out to his parents to make certain they were aware of his communication and the desperate tone it took.

His wise parents confronted him, and he assured them he had no plans of hurting himself but had voiced those things in a desperate moment. His father responded by saying he understood what it felt like to love someone and the fear of thinking about life without that person. He met his son with so much empathy and attunement. He helped his son imagine what kind of pressure and responsibility his girlfriend must have felt in carrying his words.

This dad had challenged his son to journal in the past, and had even bought him a journal as a gift. He encouraged him to use the journal now as a place to record his thoughts and feelings. He'd reminded his son it would be tempting to use texting for that purpose if he didn't have a safe place to channel all those thoughts and emotions.

He told his son what he put in the texts would have been perfect for his journal. He could have gone back to his thoughts at a later point to identify if that was still his current state of being. This wise dad said, "I hope you will always write it down [in a journal, not texts]. Moving those thoughts and feelings *outward* is a good idea 100 percent of the time. Otherwise, they can stay trapped inside and almost become cancerous to our system." He went on to ask some great questions that helped his son connect the dots to see how he'd used his girlfriend as a way of working through his fear, rather than doing the work himself.

His dad went on to help him differentiate between using a person as *support* and using them to *regulate*. I have this conversation often in my office. It's vital that boys learn the skills to calm their bodies and brains alone. Training boys to always need a person present to do the work of regulation does two things. First, it causes them to believe they are incapable of doing the work alone. Second, it puts a tremendous amount of unnecessary responsibility on their future friends, spouses, and possibly even children. It sets the stage for the pattern of anchoring we just discussed. Anchoring is lazy emotional work. Journaling is effortful.

Boys are quick to answer "I don't know" to questions that involve them having to think or reflect. Writing it down forces them to develop their thoughts and, in turn, to become more psychologically minded. I talk often about the importance of helping boys build a psychological immune system.

Think of the first time you took your son to the pediatrician for a cold or virus. The doctor or nurse likely said something like, "Well, at least his immune system is getting stronger." We all know that when the body is fighting off disease of any kind, the immune system is strengthened in the process.

The same is true when kids face difficult circumstances, navigate challenging emotions, or problem-solve their way through a hurdle in life. They are developing a more robust psychological immune system in these moments.

Journaling allows kids to develop in this way. It's a tool to process their emotions in a thoughtful way, reframe difficult circumstances, build their self-esteem and understanding of themselves, think backward and forward, and clear their thoughts before bedtime.

I have a friend who is a social work professor at a university. As the pandemic of 2020 continued, I asked what she was seeing in her students. She commented they seemed to be weathering the pandemic with more resilience simply because they had skills in place that other students didn't. She required each of them to journal as a weekly graded assignment. Within the journaling experience, they had to develop a self-care plan and identify coping skills that were currently working for them.

This practice was something she'd used for as long as she'd been teaching. It wasn't new to COVID-19; it was a long-term plan in place that happened to serve her students in a unique way during a particularly difficult time in their lives.

We want our sons to be equipped like these students for however they experience life on life's terms.

Effortless vs. Effortful

It's important to note here that journaling requires effort. It's easier not to write anything down. Just as it's easier to say "I don't know" in response to questions. It's easier to melt down than it is to develop practices that calm my nervous system.

The work of regulation is effortful. It's never effortless. And it's vital in raising emotionally strong boys. No different from the way building physical muscles involves work—strength training and conditioning. No human ever got physically fit by lying on a couch.

Thankfully most boys understand training. They also understand the concept of a coach. There's not a professional athlete who trained himself. Every successful athlete had invested coaches standing on the sidelines giving instruction and feedback.

This emotional training is no different. Boys need coaching and practice. If he can't receive instruction and feedback well from you as his parents, you may need to engage an outside source. Many boys will resist that kind of training, but I'd argue it's not just important, it's necessary.

Happiness vs. Character

I laughed with some parents in a consultation last week. Their son had worked with an ADHD coach as a fourth grader following his diagnosis. He was open at first and resistant at the end. They stopped the process and tried again with a new therapist in middle school. By the time they reached out to me, they had worked with six different clinicians (learning specialists, ADHD coaches, child and adolescent therapists and psychiatrists). The dad commented that he believed they "simply haven't marketed it the right way to pique our son's interest."

I told him I doubted it was his marketing plan, but his son's resistance to doing the work. The majority of boys and adolescent males who walk through the front door of our counseling practice are somewhere between hesitant and resistant. I've come to believe most boys view counseling the way men view colonoscopies. Everyone knows it's a good thing to do, but no one is interested in doing it. Both feel invasive and like someone is "all up in your business."

We laughed together for a moment over that analogy, and then I challenged the parents to take the focus off the marketing and put it on their son's well-being. I've found we spend a lot of energy pursuing our kids' happiness at the expense of their well-being. I challenged them to communicate this clearly to their son. To let him know they heard his voice and were aware he was disinterested in meeting with anyone, but it was no longer his decision alone.

The circumstances that brought them into our time included a volatile exchange on the basketball court with an opponent, yelling at a teacher in class, countless explosive episodes at home, and a call from school that he'd told a classmate he was considering killing himself.

This young man, like many boys, had limited emotional skills in place. He was nearing his sixteenth birthday, and his parents had significant concerns about putting this explosive, impulsive, dysregulated kid behind the wheel of a car. I raised their concern with my own concern that if he didn't develop some skills soon, he would likely find his way to substances as a means of medicating his pain. He'd already developed a habit of medicating with screens and would frequently fly off the handle when asked to turn off his phone, iPad, or gaming system.

I developed the conversation more around prioritizing well-being and invited his parents to see this decision as no different from taking him to well visits at the pediatrician, the dentist for cleanings, or tutoring in the summers. There's not a living, breathing kid who begs to go to the doctor for shots or finger pricks, or the dentist for plaque removal. However, we take kids we love to these appointments because we know it's connected to their overall well-being.

Prioritizing well-being over happiness is a mark of love.

Loving parents don't allow underage kids to abuse substances, because it's dangerous and illegal. Similarly, we set limits, require chores, enforce boundaries, and offer discipline because we wisely know that these things create safety and security for developing people. We don't do it because it makes kids happy. We do it because it makes them healthy. Prioritizing well-being over happiness is a mark of love.

Or have you forgotten how good parents treat children, and that God regards you as *his* children?

My dear child, don't shrug off God's discipline,
but don't be crushed by it either.
It's the child he loves that he disciplines;
the child he embraces, he also corrects.

God is educating you; that's why you must never drop out. He's treating you as dear children. This trouble you're in isn't punishment; it's *training*, the normal experience of children. Only irresponsible parents leave children to fend for themselves. Would you prefer an irresponsible God? We respect our own parents for training and not spoiling us, so why not embrace God's training so we can truly *live*? While we were children, our parents did what *seemed* best to them. But God is doing what *is* best for us, training us to live God's holy best. At the time, discipline isn't much fun. It always feels like it's going against the grain. Later, of course, it pays off big-time, for it's the well-trained who find themselves mature in their relationship with God.

Hebrews 12:5–11 The Message

Goal Setting

Attending to our kids' well-being involves creating contexts for them to continue to develop their strengths while also helping them develop in areas of weakness.

Years ago I joined a gym, and part of the package included three free sessions with a trainer. I'd never had a personal trainer in my life and thought it would be fun to have that experience. Especially if I didn't have to pay extra for it. I remember arriving for my training session early like a kid on his first day of kindergarten. The trainer was easily twenty years younger and clearly in better shape. He began the session with some questions about my health history. The more questions he asked, the more insecure I felt about the experience. I was certain he could tell by my appearance that I was a middle-aged father of three, but I made sure to state the obvious, to confirm he'd set low expectations and move at a beginner's pace.

Twenty minutes into the workout, I announced I was about to throw up. I remember splashing cold water on my face in the sink and thinking, *Why would anyone pay money for this torture?* I would revisit that thought the day after my second "free" session, when my muscles were as sore as they'd been in my life.

My body was crying out for relief because I was working weak muscles. Though I hope the work of building emotional muscles doesn't bring about the same kind of agony, it's important to note that our sons may struggle greatly in the working of their weaker muscles.

I mentioned the work of regulation, because, again, it's work. Unlike my trainer on the first visit, I'd encourage you to pace the work according to your son's skills and temperament. As you're setting goals, do your best to make them *measurable* and *manageable*.

I do a good amount of goal setting with boys in my office. Their tendency is often to set big, challenging goals. While I appreciate a boy's desire to push himself, I often find it comes from having little practice with goal setting. Many people struggle with goals because they simply set the goal line too far away in the early attempts.

Many who want to begin running challenge themselves to sign up for a marathon, rather than a fun run or a 5K. Running 26.2 miles is a long distance if you're a beginner. Consider starting with a 5K and then move to a 10K, run a few half marathons, and then attempt a full marathon. Meeting smaller goals increases our desire to keep pushing forward. It also allows us to see small successes along the way.

In the same way, boys struggle to set goals that can be easily measured. Many boys struggling in school write down goals like "work harder" or "study more," as opposed to goals like "make all Bs and above" or "study math facts for fifteen extra minutes a night." Goals could include engaging a tutor two afternoons a week, spending two hours on ACT prep every

Saturday morning, or taking three practice ACT tests. Do you see how specific these goals are, and how easily measured?

Whether setting physical, emotional, relational, or spiritual goals, boys will need coaching in how to set goals that are both measurable and manageable as they continue casting a vision for themselves. Goal setting has been linked to resilience and a growth mindset. It has endless layers of benefit when done well.

Casting a Vision

The other benefit of helping boys develop goals is it trains them to cast a vision for where they hope to be. I've sat with countless boys in their junior and senior years of high school who can't articulate anything about what they want the next chapter of life to look like. I'm not talking about what they will be doing in twenty years; I'm talking about life after high school. They don't know if they are college bound, moving into the work force, joining the military, or taking a gap year. I don't have any expectation that a young man between sixteen and eighteen would have his entire future mapped out. I'm not even concerned for a young man who is unsure where he'd want to go to college or what he'd hope to study. It's just good to have a general sense of where he'd like to head next.

Where there is no vision, the people perish.

Proverbs 29:18 KJV

I believe boys crave purpose. It's hardwired into who we are as males. Boys lacking in purpose are vulnerable to so many things. From toddlerhood to young adulthood, we want to help boys find their way to purpose—within our families and homes, in their school and church communities, through athletic and extracurricular experiences, and within the context of their relationships. Boys are mission minded.

Goal setting not only trains boys to think forward and cast a vision for themselves, but it moves them toward purpose and allows them to tap in to their strength and capacity.

I spent time with a father recently who shared about a father-son experience with a group of men and their adolescent sons. They went away for an overnight camping experience and a time of growing together. I believe wrapping a growth experience around enjoyment is always a win. Camping, water parks, amusement parks, overnights in a hotel, movies, concerts, and so on. Anything that includes learning and laughter, conversation and connection, experience and enjoyment.

The overnight started with a massive bonfire and dinner. They played some flashlight tag and then had a time of sharing.

The next day held a hike, a trust walk, and a scavenger hunt, mixed with activities the fathers and sons did together alongside rich conversation and honest sharing.

Many of the sons reported hearing stories they'd never heard. Most of the fathers wept at some point during the weekend, and the boys had an opportunity to see emotions residing in the lives of men. They saw men being vulnerable, sharing stories of heartache and hope, regret and redemption.

Each father and son pair was given a piece of paper divided into four parts. They called it the four quadrants. In the top two squares, they were invited to describe their outside self and inside self. The outside self was a summary of how most people would describe them. The things they do and what seems obvious to the world. The inside self would include things less obvious or unknown—fears and hopes, things they wanted to say but needed courage to do so. The bottom squares were for *formative experiences* in their lives, events that had shaped who they are. One past experience and one recent experience.

The fathers and sons sat around the campfire sharing the four quadrants. The sharing spilled into the next morning, and they were sent home with questions to ask each other over the next several weeks. The questions were simply a ve-hicle to keep the conversation, reflection, and dialogue going.

This is something any parent, grandparent, youth pas-tor, or mentor could do. It could be the jumping off point for starting a book club or small group, quarterly weekends together, or an annual trip. The key ingredients are time and intention.

Reflective exercises like this are designed to help boys develop more of an interior life. Boys need to be able to articulate the events of life that have shaped who they are. They need to develop the courage to talk about their inside selves. To name their hopes and fears, joys and sorrows. A boy's capacity to do this interior work is what sets the stage for him to be present in friendships and some day marriage and parenting. If a boy can't show up to his own life, it will be extremely difficult for him to show up for others. If he can't see a reflective life on a man he respects and trusts, it will be challenging for him to develop this skill set for him-self. I'll keep gently reminding you the best way to help him develop emotional muscles is seeing the adults around him use their own.

INTENTIONAL PRACTICES

1. **Journal prompts.** *A favorite memory. A time I felt afraid. A hope for the future. If I could have any superpower. My favorite thing about summer. Three interesting facts about me. A character from a book or movie I'd like to meet and why.*

2. **Strengths assessment.** Draw a line down the center of a piece of paper. List strengths on one side and weaknesses on the other. Consider using the lists to help develop some goals.

3. **Content/discontent.** List three things you're content with and three things you are discontent with in this season of life.

4. **Highs and lows.** Take turns around the dinner table identifying great and hard moments from the day.

5. **Psalm 27:13.** Read this passage and have each family member share where they've seen evidence of the goodness of God in the recent past or present.

4

Anxiety and Depression

At the beginning of an appointment with a new family, we take kids on a tour of the Daystar office. We offer them a snack or beverage, they meet some of the therapy dogs, and we end up in one of our offices talking about why they came. We want to first hear a student's perspective on why their family reached out to schedule the appointment. It's fascinating to hear kids of many ages articulate the reasons for coming and the needs that exist. It's common for adolescent boys to say, "I don't know" or, "It was my parents' idea."

I then ask, "What's your best guess as to why your parents set this appointment?" Recently, a boy with severe anxiety (buried under years of denial) answered, "I don't know." He was noticeably frustrated to be having the conversation with me, and furious his parents had scheduled the time.

I never let boys off the hook with "I don't know." It's a lazy emotional response and evidence of underdeveloped skills.

I asked him to make a best guess, and after some resistance and stalling, he seemed to realize I wouldn't let him off the hook. He admitted he texted his dad that morning, asking why he had to come and wanting to cancel the appointment. I asked him to read the text exchange aloud to see if we could figure it out together.

Why are you making me go to counseling? His dad responded with six clear reasons. He reported multiple trips to the pediatrician for breathing and stomach issues that, after the boy was evaluated from head to toe by the pediatrician in multiple visits and scans, revealed nothing physical going on. He also reported his girlfriend frequently texted his parents to say she was worried about his "panic attacks and explosive anger." There were comments from teachers and coaches voicing concern as well. When he finished reading the list, I asked him how he felt about his dad's words.

"None of it's true," he responded.

That's a classic picture of male denial. Despite observations from his mother, father, doctor, teachers, coaches, and girlfriend, he was still reluctant to admit he had a problem. I discovered he'd previously seen three counselors for one to two appointments each and refused to go back.

I challenged his parents that it was time to stop giving him a choice in whether he thought he needed help and time to start leveraging what mattered most to him.

His dad's list also included the boy's self-medicating with alcohol and marijuana while driving. I encouraged them to drug test him and take his car keys if they discovered he was continuing to use. Despite the concerns from multiple reliable sources, they continued to let him drive and date, and they paid for his gas, insurance, and cell phone bill, and they gave him monthly spending money. He had full support and was calling the shots. Yet he was struggling greatly, and the entire family was suffering as a result of an unwillingness to get help.

While I was meeting with his parents (for approximately twenty-five minutes), he texted his dad repeatedly and then called five times when he didn't respond. His father held out his phone to show me the number of attempts and said, "This is what he does if we don't respond immediately." Anxious boys are often highly dysregulated and can't deal with the discomfort of waiting. They ask endless questions, demand input, and anchor themselves to someone who will become their resources when they haven't developed resourcefulness.

I reminded his parents the runway was short before he'd graduate, move away, and be on his own. They had a small window of time to fold in consistent support and equip him with the skills to navigate this debilitating anxiety. Soon they'd have no ownership over his process. This is the kind of young man who goes away to college and can easily move from experimentation to addiction. In an attempt to silence the anxiety or alleviate the depression, he needs more and more of a substance to numb the discomfort.

This unproductive cycle yields a harmful outcome of shame and substance abuse. He then experiences more shame from hiding the habit and lying to cover his tracks, in a way that only feeds the need for more. And the cycle continues.

Missing the Signs

This young man's anxiety is a reminder that presentation is sometimes misleading. Anxious boys often look rigid, stubborn, controlling, perfectionistic, angry, or explosive. With boys, anxiety can certainly present as fearful and worried, but more often it looks agitated and explosive. Depressed boys sometimes look sad and lethargic, but more often irritable and volatile. I once had a mom describe her depressed son as "chronically in a bad mood—a low-grade irritability he wakes up with every morning." This young man wasn't crying in bed, but screaming and oppositional.

When we consider the movement of anxiety and depression, we often think of going inward. Turning inward with worry or becoming isolated in sadness. Boys can certainly present with inward movement, but many times it's *outward* movement. Emotional outbursts full of yelling, hitting, throwing, and threatening.

My counseling experience tells me a percentage of boys (often firstborns) demonstrate the more classic presentation of perfectionism, control, and over-performing as a means of managing anxiety. Their depression is more of an anger turned inward that drives a need to please and perform, both academically and athletically. This presentation, wherever a young man falls in birth order, results in boys who blur the line between excellence and perfection. They set the bar of performance at an unreasonable place, requiring impossible things of themselves in an effort to outrun the difficult emotions they are experiencing.

Interestingly enough, over-performing is a dressed-up version of numbing out. An inability to deal with the discomfort of life drives a need to shut down the internal storm with external performance. To the degree that I feel out of control internally, I will work to try to control something externally—people, outcomes, situations, or circumstances. It's an attempt to quiet a storm that's raging inside. The louder the storm, the more desperate the need for control.

Signals and Sirens

I talk with boys about how a car's dashboard is designed to signal us in how to best care for the vehicle. We get a warning signal when a tire is low, the oil needs changing, or routine maintenance is required. As long as we respond to the signal in a timely manner by adding air to a tire, changing the oil, or capping off the wiper fluid, the car will run well.

If we get a check engine light, it may be an indicator of a larger internal issue. Depending on the vehicle, it may simply be time for a service appointment, *or* it may be an indicator of a greater need requiring attention. Boys need to know our bodies work in the same way. We have internal signals and sirens alerting us to something needing attention. Your body may signal you with an increased heart rate, tightness in your back or other muscles, sensations in your stomach, or tension in your head. There are many ways our bodies fire off emotional flares in a physical presentation.

Emotions are like the tire, oil, or wiper fluid lights. They alert us to experiences worth paying attention to throughout our day. Anxiety and depression are more like the check engine light, an indicator that more may be going on.

We all know ignoring a check engine light for an extended period can result in significant damage to the vehicle. There could be an internal issue that, left unattended, could harm the operating system.

To stay with this analogy a bit longer, I often explain that sometimes we can attend to the vehicle on our own. I know how to put air in the tires and top off wiper fluid. Some men know how to change the oil themselves. Yet, often times, we need a mechanic to weigh in—someone with expertise to help us assess the problem and determine a path forward.

> **Getting help isn't a sign of weakness— it's a sign of wisdom.**

Most men are happy to turn their vehicle over to a mechanic. Fewer men are happy to turn their well-being over to a professional such as a counselor, doctor, or pastor. Getting input from an outside source is a wise and responsible thing to do. It's an acknowledgment that I can't possibly know everything there is to know about something. Getting help isn't a sign of weakness—it's a sign of wisdom. In my opinion, putting another set of eyes on the situation is a sign of intelligence, not incompetence.

Naming/Breathing/Coping

My work with young men always starts with naming/breathing/coping. These are the ABCs of emotional work. As basic and simple as they sound, I can't begin to tell you how many males I know who don't have these foundational building blocks in place. Just as learning the building blocks of reading can take longer for some kids than others, learning the building blocks of emotions can be more labor-intensive for some boys.

Development, temperament, and modeling certainly impact the equation. The further a boy is into his development, the harder it can be to teach him these skills. Just as we all know it's easier to learn a new instrument or a second language when you're younger, the same is true with this type of learning. I'm an advocate for beginning this work as early as possible in a boy's life, with the reminder that it's never too late. Whatever age your son (or husband) may be as you're reading this book, hear me say those words again: It's never too late. It turns out you *can* teach an old dog new tricks. The learning may simply take longer.

Temperament will certainly play a role. Some boys are more open-minded and eager to learn. Some are more stubborn and less coachable. Some boys operate with more of a fixed mindset; some have developed more of a growth mindset. Some boys are glass half-full; some are glass half-empty. Your job is simply to lean into all of what God is revealing to you about your son's core temperament and the direction he seems to naturally bend. Acknowledge his temperament as you teach these skills.

If a boy is parented by adults with limited emotional vocabularies and no healthy coping skills in place, he simply hasn't had the opportunity to see enough modeling. You'll be learning along with him, and I'd encourage you to be vocal about how you are *all* learning together. I think it's great when boys hear parents acknowledge they didn't grow up voicing feelings and have some catch-up work to do.

Naming

Naming feelings is easier done with a feelings chart in hand. It turns fill-in-the-blank into multiple choice. Boys no longer have to come up with the emotion. They can simply reference the chart for ideas. My challenge to parents is to watch for as many opportunities as possible (at the dinner table, during car time, family walks, weekend hikes) to fold emotional vocabulary into your daily conversations as you share life together and report on the events of life.

Breathing

Deep breathing is a foundational, well-researched practice for calming the brain and body. Early in my work with any boy, I'll arm him with the skill of relaxation breathing. I begin with some basic education about the brain. I talk about how there's blood flow moving throughout our brains, and when we are calm most of that is hovering around our prefrontal cortex, which houses our frontal lobes. Our frontal lobes help us

1. think rationally and
2. manage our emotions.

When we are emotionally charged, anxious, or worried, the blood flow moves to the back of the brain to the amygdala. The amygdala is the part of the brain that triggers a fight, flight, or freeze response. At that point, we are at a heightened state of arousal. Our job is to get the blood flow back to the front of the brain so we can think rationally and manage our emotions. Breathing is the most efficient and effective way to create that backward-to-forward movement.

Over the years I've done work with Navy SEALs, Army Rangers, and Special Forces members and their families. While talking about this concept, one of them called it **combat breathing**. They went on to share it was a necessary skill set as they'd inevitably find themselves in life-or-death situations and needing to calm their brain and body to make thoughtful, rational, strategic decisions. I liked the sound of "combat breathing" better than "deep breathing" for boys. I appreciated how it spoke to the battle going on in our brains and bodies and the fight for rational thinking and regulated emotions.

I walk boys through one to three minutes of combat breathing, asking them at the end what they feel and about any differences they notice in their body. I wear an Apple watch and will have boys take a look at my heart rate before the breathing starts and again once it ends. Consistently I can lower my heart rate with only a few minutes of combat breathing. This serves as hard evidence of the benefit any one of us can experience in mastering this skill that can be used anywhere, anytime. I have boys use it before a timed test, in the dugout, on the free throw line, before a fine arts performance, when asking a girl to a dance, or during a hard conversation with parents. The benefits are endless.

Coping Skills

Developing coping skills is the next step in equipping boys. I have young men of all ages leave my office with a Top Five List—a list of outlets for taking the emotion to something constructive. I mentioned earlier that boys have a lot of physicality to their emotions. As a result of this, I want the list to include some physical releases like shooting hoops, walking the dog, running laps, jumping on the trampoline, pull-ups or push-ups, and lunges or sit-ups. The Space discussed in chapter 2 could be a great place to hang the Top Five List for a point of reference.

I often teach some grounding techniques for anchoring themselves to the present when the emotions thrust them into the past or future. Anxiety resides in the past or future. It's worry over something that has already happened or could happen in the future. Ruminating and forecasting are benchmarks of anxiety. Grounding techniques allow boys to get back to the present.

Techniques include counting backward, identifying everything in the room of a certain color, or walking oneself through the five senses and acknowledging things they currently can see, smell, hear, taste, and touch. These are cognitive tasks that occupy the brain when it's spinning off into worry or hopelessness. These practices are well-researched strategies within cognitive-behavioral therapy that boys can do anytime and anywhere.

One rule I have when helping boys of any age create a Top Five List is "no screens." As I've mentioned before, screens are an escape, not a strategy. As a boy becomes skilled in naming/breathing/coping, I'm open to letting him add the Calm, Pause, or Headspace app to his arsenal, but in the beginning it's simply too easy to start with that app and end up mindlessly scrolling. Using the app is like graduate-level work. We only begin grad school after completing undergrad.

Naming/breathing/coping is the beginning work to help any young man fight against anxiety or depression. It's important to note here that any parent can work with their son on these basic strategies. For a percentage of boys, these skills may be enough to begin the battle against worry and anxiety, despair and depression. For another percentage, they need another voice and outside support in the mix—a professional who can come alongside a boy and his parents to address the symptoms. Other boys may also need medication as part of the journey. Engaging a pediatrician or psychiatrist can be a helpful and necessary step for young men who need an additional layer of support.

Not only do I recommend parents be open to outside support, but I encourage you to be positive about it. Talk about the benefits, name the gift of having access to mental health resources, and discuss the advantage of living at a time in history when we understand mental health to be as important as physical health.

If you're unsure where your son is in his emotional journey, I strongly recommend you begin with a consultation with his pediatrician or a trained clinician. A screening or evaluation may be needed to accurately assess the symptoms and circumstances. When in doubt, lean into support. Not only does it give you peace of mind as a parent raising sons at a time in history when boys lead some of the scariest statistics, but it defines the healthy path of asking for help when help is needed.

In my experience, it's more than possible for boys to graduate from excessive worry to full-blown anxiety or from sadness to self-harm at an accelerated pace. Let's get out in front of as much as possible on behalf of the boys we love. Let's err on the side of more support rather than less.

Depression and Suicide

Not long ago I read a story about a man, Devon Levesque, who lost his father to suicide when he was only sixteen. His father's suicide took place in the aftermath of a divorce and the 2008 financial crash.

Levesque decided to complete the New York City Marathon to raise awareness of mental health and to raise monetary support for veterans.

His story caught the attention of media outlets everywhere because he didn't just choose to run the marathon, which is a feat in itself, but to bear crawl. Yes, you read that correctly. He chose to bear crawl for 26.2 miles. I'd challenge you to bear crawl one lap around your house. Experience how uncomfortable it is to move any distance in that position, and then what your back feels like when you stand up.

I was struck by the discipline and agony he'd endure in training alone, much less completing the race.

I was encouraged by his desire to bring attention to mental health. His grandfather and father were both body builders. Levesque himself is a wellness and fitness expert. Yet, out of his story, he wants to draw attention to what it means to be both physically *and* mentally strong.[1]

I know many males who are physically strong but not mentally strong. I know countless men who are vocationally strong but not mentally strong. I've even known men who were spiritually strong but not mentally strong.

I remember one of my first exposures to suicide. It was the news of a man who was a highly successful physician. He had a beautiful wife, four young children, and a strong faith. This man was a leader in his church and widely respected in his community. He battled depression in silence and hiding. While caring for countless others in his work as a doctor, he neglected to care for himself.

He was not only a successful physician but a skilled investor. He had countless investments with an impressive portfolio. But when the market crashed, so did he. Throughout his life, he'd experienced an overwhelming amount of success and very little failure. The crash was unfamiliar territory, and like many individuals contemplating suicide, he began believing his pain exceeded his resources.

In my work, I've intersected with countless families who lost a father to suicide. Sitting in the midst of that story is some of the heaviest grief I've encountered. It's not only heartbreak and loss, it's guilt and shame, questions and fear . . . a heaviness that's hard to articulate.

Walking with families through the questions, doubts, sadness, and devastation is sacred work. It's work that played a role in why I wanted to write this book. I don't want another boy, adolescent male, or man to ever believe his pain exceeds his resources. I want boys to have skills, tools, relationships, and resources.

Dr. Benita Chatmon, writing for the *American Journal of Men's Health*, says, "Depression and suicide are ranked as a leading cause of death among men. Six million men are impacted by depression in the United States every single year."[2] And on average, one man dies by suicide every minute.[3]

The Movember Foundation, a global community and charity fighting for men's health, reports,

Men are often reluctant to openly discuss their health or how they feel about the impact of significant life events;

Men are more reluctant to take action when they don't feel physically or mentally well, and;

Men engage in more risky activities that are harmful to their health.

They go on to say, "These behaviours are strongly linked to . . . traditional masculinity. Men often feel pressure to appear strong and stoic," they resist support and help,[4] and they experience greater amounts of hopelessness and despair.

Anxiety and depression are more common in girls, adolescent females, and adult women. Yet women are more likely to acknowledge a struggle and seek support. Despite lower numbers among males, it's no surprise to find depression and suicide are ranked as the leading causes of death among men, or that one man dies by suicide every minute of every day.

We have to push against this reality on behalf of the boys we love. We want to do everything in our power to raise boys who understand struggle is part of being human. Struggle is something we've been promised throughout Scripture.

"In this world you will have trouble. But take heart! I have overcome the world."

John 16:33

We know that the whole creation has been groaning as in the pains of childbirth right up to the present time.

Romans 8:22

Not only so, but we also glory in our sufferings, because we know that suffering produces perseverance; perseverance, character; and character, hope.

Romans 5:3–4

Name and Navigate

In life we've been promised struggle, but we've also been guaranteed hope. It's not one or the other. It's both. If struggle is part of the equation, we need to equip boys to name and navigate it. According to the statistics, we still have a ways to go. We are working toward expression with depression, and words with worry. It's not what comes out of us that makes us ill, it's what stays in us.

Boys are more likely to identify what they *think* rather than state what they *feel*. It's important we break this down. Help them recognize how often they answer the question of "What are you feeling?" with a *thought* rather than an emotion. It's important to understand our thoughts. Thoughts inform emotions. Emotions inform behaviors. All three are connected but separate. Unless I understand the interplay between the three, I can get roadblocked for a lifetime.

What are you thinking?

What are you feeling?

What do you want to do?

These three basic questions can help boys differentiate and determine a path forward. Keep in mind two important rules of engagement as we consider asking these questions of the boys and adolescent young men in our lives.

1. It will take time and practice for boys to answer well. These emotional muscles need both to grow and develop.

2. He can only answer these questions well when the blood flow is hovering around the prefrontal cortex,

allowing him to think rationally and manage his emotions.

Reversing the Order

If we attempt to ask these questions in an emotionally charged moment, it's like arguing with a drunk. He isn't sober minded and therefore can't answer thoughtfully. Breathing and coping often come before naming in these moments. I understand that means getting the ABCs out of order, but that's a common sequence of events. I'll continue going back to that throughout this book. Coping, and calming, comes first. When it comes to boys, rather than ABC (Naming/Breathing/Coping), it's more likely CBA (Coping/Breathing/Naming).

Reversing the sequence of events can change the game for boys and parents. Doing so honors a boy's development and creates fewer battles for parents. I'm not saying it works perfectly every time, but I'm convinced it yields a higher degree of success, alongside a higher degree of understanding.

Writing and Reflecting

When my kids were in elementary school, they were often given assignments involving journaling. Obviously these assignments were designed to develop their writing skills. I always believed their writing skills were secondary to the emotional skills being developed. When my daughter was in first grade, every student kept a yearlong journal. They could simply write about their feelings and experiences, or work with a daily journal prompt provided by the classroom teacher if they felt stuck. Their teacher would write back to them, and it became this thoughtful exchange and sacred space for conversation and connection. At the end of the year, the teacher would send each student home with the journal. It was both a time capsule from the year and a reminder of shared relationship.

I remember my daughter sharing her journal with us, and I wept as I read months of conversations, revealing more about her interior world and how she experienced what was happening around her. It remains one of my favorite keepsakes from her childhood.

Every one of us could benefit from journaling. I shared in the last chapter that I'm on a mission to bring back journaling, particularly as kids spend more time posting, tweeting, and texting. They are putting their first thoughts out into the world rather than working through thoughts and feelings in long-form writing. Journaling allows them space to work through thoughts, feelings, and ideas in a more responsive way, while technology allows for a more reactive posture.

Dialectical behavior therapy (DBT) was developed in the 1980s, and it's an evidence-based modality for treating mood disorders, suicidal ideation, and behavioral patterns like self-harm and substance abuse.

DBT argues there are three states of mind, which are the reasonable mind (logical and rational), emotional mind (moods and sensations), and wise mind (thinking and feeling). The wise mind involves the integration of the reasonable mind and the emotional mind.

To try a little DBT at home, write down three main thoughts about a situation. Follow that by writing down feelings, physical symptoms, or sensations in the body. Lastly, journal over the decisions made or actions you chose from the thoughts and emotions (healthy or unhealthy, constructive or destructive). The goal of DBT is to balance logic and emotions to create more positive outcomes when you encounter stress. The objective is to make stronger connections between thoughts, feelings, and actions.

Whether he struggles with excessive worry, intense sadness, anxiety, or depression, any boy can benefit from making connections between thoughts, feelings, and behaviors. Journaling can be a tool for helping boys form stronger connections in this area.

Four-Legged Stool

One way we can help boys integrate truth into these connections is with a practice I call the four-legged stool. I have a stool in my office that I pull out as a visual tool. I ask boys to sit on the stool and to confirm it's sturdy. Once they do, I ask how they'd feel about me removing three of the four legs. They look at me like it's a trick question, and then we laugh together about the idea of sitting on a one-legged stool. Or even a two-legged stool, for that matter. Most boys report being open to trying a three-legged stool but say all four legs would offer the best chance of not toppling over.

I hand them a piece of paper and have them write these four words:

Think

Feel

Do

True

We then work with an actual story they've told me of a moment that yielded a less-than-desirable outcome. I have them identify what they were thinking and feeling as the first two legs of the stool and then what they did in response to the thoughts or feelings.

We often discover there are multiple thoughts and feelings, and sometimes many actions, in response. For example, one young boy recently talked about doing homework at the dining room table. He hit some hard math and declared, "I can't do this. I hate math!" He then started to swing between blame and shame. "My teacher can't teach this in a way I understand." When his mom attempted to help out, he yelled, "You have no idea what you're doing. You're not even teaching it the right way." (Blame.) He then did a strong swing in the other direction. "I'm such an idiot!" Then came, "Everyone knows I'm the dumbest guy in the class." (Shame.) Those thoughts (the first leg) came back-to-back in a matter of minutes.

We then moved to the emotions (second leg) and wrote down feeling frustrated, scared, and hopeless.

For his actions (the third leg), he reported making negative statements, yelling at his mom when she offered to help, and throwing a textbook.

At this point, I have boys counter the thoughts, feelings, and actions with some truth (the fourth leg). With some distance from the experience (time and space), I have them write down what's actually true about themselves and the situation. This young man wrote,

I'm good at math, but sometimes it frustrates me.
I made a 98 on my last math test.

I'm not dumb, because I'm in the highest reading group.

My mom is always willing to help if I ask for it.

I should take a brain break every thirty minutes.

I stopped him after the first five truths. We could have gone on for a long time.

I saw another teenaged boy who was cut from a team at tryouts. He sped home teary, walked in the door, threw his backpack across the kitchen, yelled at his mother when asked about his day, and kicked an Amazon delivery across the dining room.

I walked him through this same exercise and with some distance from the situation. These were the truths he listed:

I shouldn't drive when I'm emotionally charged.

Being cut from a team means my school is full of great athletes.

I've made plenty of teams in the past.

I'm not defined by my athleticism but as a son of God.

Males tie their identity to performance way too often.

I stopped him after five truths as well. It's important to note that both of these boys had been working with this practice for some time. In fact, I'm convinced either of them could walk through the practice of the four-legged stool without having to write it down at this point, but they benefit from becoming as well-versed in the practice as possible. Otherwise, it's easy for boys to short-cut every leg of the stool.

A simple practice like this allows boys to develop more insight into the connections between their thoughts, feelings, and behaviors. It reminds them to anchor themselves to truth, rather than be driven by what they think and feel. It takes work to develop this kind of insight and skill in battling intrusive thoughts and intense emotions.

Recognize. Regulate. Repair.

As you've heard me say before, and I'll continue to say throughout this book, it's some of the most important work we do on behalf of the boys we love. I call it weight training for life.

INTENTIONAL PRACTICES

1. **Four-legged stool.** Walk boys through this integrated practice. Boys who are young can draw pictures or report their answers to you to be recorded in a notebook for reference.

2. **Grounding techniques.** Revisit the color game, counting game, and 5-4-3-2-1 (working through the five senses) as a way of anchoring back to the present when the mind is racing to past and future fears.

3. **Combat breathing.** Have him practice deep breathing, focusing on long breaths in and slow breaths out. Let him practice with a watch or heart rate monitor that allows him to see evidence of how his heart rate slows with repeated attempts.

4. **Sirens and signals.** Have him make a list of the ways his body sounds an alarm to stress, anxiety, or depression. What are the indicator lights unique to his hardwiring?

5. **Seek help.** When in doubt, begin with a consultation with his pediatrician or a therapist. We'd rather layer in too much support than too little when it comes to the possibility of something like anxiety or depression.

5

Moms and Dads

I met with the delightful parents of a four-year-old girl and six-year-old boy. They described both children as having BIG emotions with BIG responses. The mom reported seeing herself in both the kids. During a recent visit, her own mother laughed with her one morning about the wisdom of how apples don't fall far from trees. She was flashing back to a dozen moments with her own child as she watched her grandchildren navigate their emotional journeys.

The father grew up an only child and felt puzzled by the sibling rivalry. He openly and honestly admitted to struggling with regulation and being easily triggered by their conflict and meltdowns.

We talked about the Space, and what it would look like to test-drive this practice with consistency. They both agreed it could be helpful for the entire family. We talked about using a feelings chart and several other practices based on where their kids were developmentally. They came back in for a follow-up consultation three months later. I asked if they'd had a chance to try the Space, and they said they had. The kids had taken ownership and wanted to brainstorm ideas and objects for the Space. Their daughter had a bucket of art supplies, and would draw pictures of her big feelings and call them Angry Annie or Sad Susan. Their son had a mini trampoline in the Space and would jump while counting and yelling to release the intensity. I asked both parents if they'd been going there with regularity to model its benefit.

The dad laughed and said, "She sends me there all the time." His wife nodded in agreement. He continued, "After ten years of marriage, she knows me like the back of her hand. She can tell the kind of day I've had when I walk through the front door." Frequently his wife would say, "Kids, I can tell Daddy had a stressful day. He's going to spend a few minutes in the Space, and then he'll join us for dinner."

Because he loves and trusts his wife, he was letting her send him there with regularity, and it was benefitting him greatly.

He went on to tell about a time two weeks before our first appointment when he got stuck in traffic after work, arrived home late, raced in the door to catch the last part of dinner, and joined his family. His animated son was midway through telling a story about his day when he accidentally knocked over a glass of milk that spilled all over the table. The dad went off the rails. In tears he said to me, "I'm 100 percent certain I shamed this boy I love. Over spilled milk. All because I have never developed skills around what to do with my own anger." He went on to say how excited he was for his kids to see him doing this work in front of them. "We came here for the kids, but I have as much work to do as anyone."

I love his awareness. I respect his honesty. *We* are growing right alongside our kids. They aren't the only ones moving through development. Parenting is hard work that leads to good growth.

Moms

Parents are the foundation of the house. The safe relationships that allow kids to develop identity, purpose, and meaning. It's where kids see what it looks like to name and navigate emotions.

Helping boys develop emotionally and socially requires a good amount of work on the part of parents. Earlier I shared the story of the toddler following his mom around the house, melting down each time he had an audience. That pattern of anchoring is instinctive for boys. And it will continue to be their emotional and relational strategy unless we set the stage for something different. I know countless adolescent boys who follow their moms around the house trying to negotiate and argue. I once had an eighth grader say, "I'll wear her down eventually." He'd come to understand that if he stayed in the argument long enough, she'd eventually grow tired of the back-and-forth and give in to his request. This pattern is not only dangerous for a mother-son relationship, but it can train a boy to use all relationships with females to diminish his discomfort.

I call it emotional tug-of-war. Many under-resourced boys fall back on this emotional and relational strategy. It keeps them from having to problem-solve their way out of difficult emotions and circumstances. Boys who bend toward emotional tug-of-war need skilled parents who learn to drop the rope. Dropping the rope could look like saying, "I love you too much to argue. We are done talking for now." Or, "I've given you an answer, but not one you like. I'm going to head to my room to let you work through the emotions in whatever way you need to." Or, "I can tell you are struggling with my response. I'm here to support you, but not to be your punching bag."

Whatever the response, let's start with empathy and then move toward questions or boundaries as a way of setting the stage for resourcefulness. Remember that when one person drops the rope, the game of tug-of-war is over. Whether the other party likes it or not, you can always choose to set the rope down and walk away. That process can be done with empathy and support, boundaries and strength, love and wisdom.

We don't have to throw the rope to the ground, but drop it gently with care and compassion. When we don't develop this skill, boys will seek to keep us playing tug-of-war for endless periods of time as a way of avoiding emotions, problem-solving, and moving toward healthy coping skills.

Think of it a bit like sleep training. Remember how difficult it was to swaddle him, kiss his head, set him in his crib, and then exit the room while he settled into sleep? The reason parents take on the hard work of sleep training is so that he doesn't need a person present in order to settle his brain and body when it comes to sleep. If the only way he is capable of settling himself is through rocking, nursing, or being held, he never learns the early skills of self-soothing, a benchmark of regulation.

Years ago, I consulted with a mom who chose a family bed, nursed on demand, and reported she had never completed a phone call "without him interrupting me with a need." By the time this boy turned eight, he'd come to treat her like an ATM. He would make withdrawals 24/7. When he experienced a need of any kind, he would wake her, yell for her, demand of her, or require she come immediately.

> **When one person drops the rope, the game of tug-of-war is over.**

She reported parenting him was like having a fifty-pound infant attached to her at all times. He had endless needs and zero skills.

It's vital we interrupt the patterns of anchoring as a boy grows and develops. We want him to do the important work of regulation. If he can't settle himself during his sleep and awake time, or during moments of fear or frustration, he will be ill-equipped to navigate the discomfort of life.

Blame and Shame

As we've discussed, the other place boys commonly get stuck in their relationships with moms is with blame. In the face of failure or disappointment, boys tend to point the finger at others before pointing it back at themselves. I've heard thousands of examples of this over the years, blaming mothers, teachers, coaches, girlfriends, siblings, classmates, and friends.

When boys can't find a lost item, they blame their moms for not putting it in the right place rather than considering they may have misplaced it themselves.

When they bomb a test, they blame their teachers for not teaching it the right way rather than admitting they may not have studied or prepared enough.

When they don't get the playing time they wanted, they blame their coaches for not preparing them rather than recognizing they may not have practiced enough.

When they are called out for sibling conflict, they blame their sibling for starting it rather than owning their contribution.

The list goes on and on. Boys tend to swing between blame and shame. They have a hard time getting to the healthy middle.

Blame  Ownership Shame

Blame looks like "It's your fault," or "She made me do it," or "He didn't prepare me," or "She has it out for me."

Shame looks like "I'm such an idiot," or "I'm the worst member of this family," or "I should just die," or "I don't deserve to live."

Neither blame nor shame is healthy. Neither is helpful. Both keep him from healthy ownership and cleaning up his side of the street. Blame involves deflection and avoidance. Shame involves self-contempt and sabotage. Neither moves him toward restoration or resolution.

Healthy ownership typically starts with moving the blood flow from the back to the front. That process of regulation that allows him to think rationally and manage his emotions. Once he's in a more settled state, consider using the above diagram with him and help him make connections around his swing. Some boys only move toward blame. Some go instinctively to shame. Many boys swing back and forth between both. It can be helpful to have him write down some of the blame and shame declarations you remember him making during the exchange.

Move from there to helping him make some different declarations that land him in the space of healthy ownership. Statements like "I didn't get the grade I wanted. I didn't prepare as well I could have." Or, "I lost my temper over the iPad, but you told me how long I had before I started and gave me a five-minute warning." Or, "I hated the outcome of the game, but I didn't spend much time practicing last week."

Statements that allow him to make connections. Declarations that anchor him to truth and ownership. Developing in this space is long work. It isn't something a boy develops mastery over in a day. For many young men, it's a good bit of two steps forward and three steps back. Progress mixed with some regression. Depending on how long he's been stuck in a pattern of anchoring, it may be fewer steps forward with more steps back. Keep the long game in mind. Continue reminding yourself, and having others remind you, of the importance of his breaking the pattern of anchoring and developing skills for coping.

Keep remembering the short- and long-term benefits of this journey. In the short term, developing in this space allows you to be a champion of his well-being and not his emotional life support. Long term, you are preparing him to have healthy relationships with all the other females in his life as opposed to using them or needing them in order to survive.

We want him to experience *satisfaction* in relationships, not *survival*. We want him to both enjoy his relationships and contribute to them. He can't do either well when he's dependent on them for survival. His relationships should add to his well-being, but not be the source of sustainability.

As you seek to support your son's developing in this way, let's look at three unique callings on the relationship between a mother and a son. I believe these callings are communicated well by Gina Bria, an anthropologist and author.

> The work of mothering a son is mostly about stepping aside with precise timing. I want my sons, both of them, to learn from me that they are free to be rooted in home and still be abroad in the world as men.[1]

1. Being Safe

Mothers play a significant role in the lives of boys. Early in a boy's journey, his mom is like the center of his universe. She is like a planet he is orbiting around at all times. Moms are the safest place on earth. I believe boys often give the most of who they are to their moms.

Unfortunately the *most* includes the best *and* the worst. As much as I wish it was only the best, it's both. Out of that safety, a mom's objective is to be a *sounding board*, not a *verbal punching bag*. Boys often confuse one for the other and can require a good amount of coaching in this area.

I think it's important for moms to say things like "I'm sorry you're in a bad mood, but that doesn't mean you get to take it out on me." Or, "I can tell you are having a hard time. What do you need?" We always want to be moving boys toward resourcefulness. A mom can be so busy being a boy's resources that there's no space for him to develop resourcefulness.

Asking him questions like "What do you need?" or, "How can I support you?" moves him toward resourcefulness. These questions also communicate we believe in who he is, and we see him as capable and competent. Problem-solving for him sends the opposite message—that he isn't capable or competent enough to move through a hard situation.

Keep in mind that as boys are developing skills, they are as vulnerable to creating a hostage crisis as they are to playing tug-of-war. I realize the language of "hostage crisis" sounds a bit strong, but I think it's accurate. Having done this work for twenty-five years, I'm fascinated by the lengths boys will go to in order to keep their moms engaged in their struggle. When the blame game fails to work, they will often swing toward shame and self-contempt in an attempt to keep them engaged. They seem to learn early on that moms can't turn away easily from statements like "I'm the worst kid," or "No one loves me."

Years ago, I worked with a mom of an incredibly bright fifteen-year-old. He was masterful in baiting his mom into emotional tug-of-war when he bumped up against discomfort of any kind. He tended to use his advanced cognitive skills in this arena, as bright boys will do. His mother came to realize she needed to go to her room and close the door to separate herself from his attempts to manipulate and bait her. She described him as "an Olympic gold medalist in manipulation." He was also prone to violating boundaries. She would say that she was going to her room and closing the door to have some space to reflect and breathe. He would open the door and walk right in without permission. She began to lock the door, and he would lean against the locked door and say, "What kind of mother won't listen to her own son?"

The irony was that she had listened to him argue, negotiate, and manipulate for more hours than any parent I'd known in my work. She came to realize there was no end to the listening. And that the listening was not about him being heard, but about her changing her mind and giving him whatever he wanted.

Just as a terrorist will trap you to meet his demands, so a boy will hold you hostage for the same purpose. There is a clear difference between listening and supporting and being held hostage for the sake of meeting his demands. It's vital to learn the difference and avoid the latter. Interrupting tug-of-war and a hostage crisis is necessary for developing a healthy mother-son relationship for boys who are low in resourcefulness and high in manipulation. Listening for blame and shame to avoid getting trapped is part of safeguarding the relationship, alongside helping him develop necessary skills.

As we've discussed in earlier chapters, many times boys can't do good problem-solving until they've released some of the physicality of the emotion and moved the blood flow back to the prefrontal cortex, where they can think rationally again. Walking him to the Space, challenging him to go, or going on our own invites resourcefulness. It also pulls mothers and sons out of emotional tug-of-war.

2. Letting Go

Moving him toward resourcefulness and helping him build skills also invites a next objective for a mom. As he moves toward adolescence and begins to do some healthy separating out, the relationship begins to change. The relationship doesn't stop; it simply needs to evolve. Boys begin to talk less and isolate more. They are often less engaged and harder to connect with in this stretch of development.

This season requires some creativity. My experience is that the separating out tends to be more clumsy than clean. Particularly when it comes to firstborn males. This is everyone's first rodeo—his and yours. For years you've been the center of his universe, and that involved mostly movement toward you, and now he's doing some moving away. I believe it's important that mothers name this transition and bless it. That happens when moms talk openly with boys about the changes they are experiencing—physically and emotionally—and how that inevitably changes things relationally. It's vital that boys hear moms say that although the relationship feels different, it doesn't mean they still can't be close and connected—they're just learning to talk and relate in different ways. It's good for a mom to learn to talk more shoulder-to-shoulder than face-to-face as a boy moves into adolescence.

Go on walks together with the family dog. Retrieve the ball while he's shooting hoops and talk at the basketball goal. Watch for where he may open up more at night, perhaps still wanting you to come in and scratch his back. Conversations in the dark can feel easier and more natural. Talk in the car and around the dinner table, and use food as a primary tool for opening him up. There really is truth in the age-old saying that the way to a man's heart is through his stomach.

You may observe him wanting to spend a bit more time around his dad, coaches, and mentors. Boys crave male attention and validation in unique ways throughout adolescence. Competing with or roadblocking this need is never helpful. This may take some significant work if divorce is a chapter in your story, or if you have a complicated, hurdled relationship with your son's father. My challenge would be to do the work you need to do to allow your son to extract and experience what he needs from his relationship with his dad.

If there are complicated elements to who his father is, your son needs to connect those dots in his own time. I've sat with too many boys over the years with moms who are filling in the blanks for them, rather than waiting on them to make those connections. I have seen it consistently breed resentment and even cause some irreparable damage to a mother-son relationship. Some boys make those connections earlier, and some refuse to make them until much further down the road. Waiting for that to happen can be incredibly difficult and even painful to watch.

Keep asking good questions. He may need you to be a sounding board in this space. Trust me when I tell you that he's *not* asking you to join him in making negative statements about his dad. He simply needs to you to listen and let him talk it through. When in doubt, keep asking questions while validating the hard work of wrestling through that he's doing. Doing so invites more resourcefulness and benefits him greatly in his future relationships.

If your son doesn't have access to his dad through loss of some kind, your job becomes praying in and ushering in other trusted male voices. This could be his grandfather, uncle, mentor, or a close friend's dad. He will need your support and blessing in bridging that space between the strength of your relationship and his need for male connection. It's helpful for him to hear you speak to not knowing all of what he will need and encounter in his journey from boyhood to manhood, and having access to a trusted male voice to get information, a place to ask questions and a context for connection is vital to his growth and development.

3. Staying Steady

This leads us to the third objective. Staying steady during the toddler tantrums and teenage turmoil can be one of the greater challenges a mom faces. Again I'd emphasize that staying steady doesn't mean you become a punching bag and tolerate his disrespect. It simply means you offer him a balance of strength and love.

Staying steady means you may be impacted by his words and emotions, but they don't inform who you are. Staying steady positions us to prioritize his well-being over his happiness.

I've long believed that staying steady is what allows us to endure finger pricks and shots at the pediatrician's office, cleanings at the dentist, standardized testing in schools, naps, bedtime, screen limits, and serving vegetables. We do all of these things, despite a great amount of pushback, because we know they're connected to our kids' greater good.

Staying steady doesn't mean we operate void of emotion. Quite the opposite. You've heard me say repeatedly that hearing you name your feelings and experiences benefits him greatly. There's a difference between naming your feelings and making him responsible for them. Boys should never feel power *over* you. They need parents to be the strongest people in the room. That doesn't mean we aren't hurt, don't have tears, or don't voice our emotions. It communicates that he doesn't have the power to create a hostage crisis that causes you to abandon his well-being and surrender to his momentary happiness.

I'm working with a mom of a sixteen-year-old boy who throws some pretty intense verbal daggers when he's emotionally charged and can be incredibly wounding in an attempt to get his needs met. His wise mother is disinterested in training him to become manipulative or aggressive as a way of getting his needs met. She will periodically remind him that she is parenting with the end goal of having a great relationship with her future daughter-in-law.

I love that. She is parenting with a long view and casting a vision for where they are headed. She realizes training him to be manipulative would make his next relationship a train wreck and likely leave her future daughter-in-law asking, "*Who raised this guy?*"

On that note, moms play a vital role in helping boys learn how to relate to the opposite sex. How a female feels respected, cherished, and honored. To the degree a mom prioritizes being safe, letting go, and staying steady, her son can grow into a healthier understanding of boundaries and relationship. Boys who use their moms as verbal punching bags often grow into men who transfer that relational strategy onto the next female in their life.

Dads

Fathers also teach boys a great deal about relationship with the opposite sex. If a boy can sit front row to a mom and dad navigating conflict in a healthy, constructive way, he lays a foundation for how relationship works. He begins learning that marriage is messy and magical. A relationship that involves two completely different people building a life together—working through differences, learning to agree to disagree, respecting perspectives, forgiving and growing, and learning to become one flesh. It's magical when this can happen. It takes tremendous sacrifice and love. Very few boys get a chance to observe this reality. Not simply because the statistics of marriages ending in divorce are so high, but also because few married couples give boys a snapshot of this kind of marriage. It's why I've challenged hundreds of parents over the years to turn their attention first to their marriage before diving deeper into parenting practices.

Boys need equal parts strength and love from their fathers as well. It's easy to slide into good cop/bad cop roles with our kids. They don't need one parent who is the disciplinarian and one who is only fun. They need connection and consequences from both parents. I challenge married and divorced parents to periodically evaluate how they are doing with balancing strength and love, connection and consequences. Parents may be able to do this as a couple, but depending on their relationship, they may benefit from including a neutral third party. Evaluate where you may need to offer more unity and consistency. Evaluate where you may need to pass the baton more frequently to allow the other parent to offer more in an area that's lacking.

Just as I challenged moms to allow boys to make connections in their own time with regard to a complicated relationship, I'd challenge dads in the same way. No boy is interested in hearing his dad speak negatively about his mom. If he is voicing frustrations about his mom, you can be a sounding board, while always pointing him back to two things:

1. How much his mom loves him. (Even if she gets roadblocked in moments that make relationship complicated.)
2. How important it is to voice those frustrations (in a respectful way) and problem-solve his way to something different.

Moving a boy in this direction honors the importance of his relationship with his mom. The research has consistently reminded us that having a healthy relationship with *both* parents makes a boy healthier. Acting as if he simply doesn't need one of the relationships will never serve him best. Years ago I was working with a twelve-year-old boy whose parents went through a high-conflict divorce. Infidelity and addiction were only a few of the ingredients involved.

When his father got sober and attempted to make amends with his ex-wife, she wouldn't allow it and resisted any conversation. She communicated to her son that whatever his dad said, it would always be followed by failed actions at some point. She was unwilling to give him space to change or be different, based on years of hurt and betrayed trust.

Each time the boy asked for additional time with his dad, it was met with strong emotion and a list of reasons why he was setting himself up for disappointment. The son found the courage one day to say, "We talk a lot about forgiveness at home and church, but you won't give it to one of the most important people in my life. Not just that, you won't allow me to have my own relationship with my dad. Every time you tell me not to go to his house, it makes me want to spend more time with him and less with you."

His words were sobering and truthful. They speak to a boy's desire to have full access to both parents. Evaluate where you could make adjustments in your parenting to better pave the way for complete access. Pay attention to how you may be making connections *for* him where he needs to do that on his own, *and* in his own time.

Validation

Boys, like men, can root their identity in performance. Consider how we begin conversations with "What do you do?" As if vocation is the most important quality about a person. We do a version of this with boys when we lead with "What sports do you play?" These aren't bad questions—we simply want to pay attention to whether we're leading with them.

For years I've challenged parents to take boys out for ice cream following a *loss* as often as a *victory*. It's one way to communicate strongly that

1. loss is a part of every person's experience,
2. we aren't defined by our performance, and
3. connection and enjoyment happen because of *who* they are, not what they do.

Celebrating after loss communicates clearly to boys that our pleasure doesn't rest in their performance, but rather seeing them do something they love. Avoid a tendency to use that time to reflect on what they did wrong or what they could have done better. Ask questions like

1. Who supported you today and how? (coach, team-mate, spectator)
2. What's a contribution you made that felt meaning-ful? (on or off the field)
3. Who did you show up for today and how?

These questions allow boys to become reflective and more psychologically minded, remind them of the importance of the experience, and anchor them to the ultimate calling all of us have on our lives—knowing God and caring for his people. This connects a boy early on to what will give his life meaning and purpose, in whatever context he may be operating.

Connection

These questions can move beyond the court and field, and we can invite boys to consider their relationships, how they are investing in them, and how they are experiencing being invested in.

Boys benefit from hearing the men in their lives talk about their friendships and the relationships and experiences that have most shaped them. I commonly ask boys to name their mom's three closest friends. Then I ask the same question about their dad. Almost every boy I know can answer the first question easily but has to think long and hard on the second. Men don't tend to prioritize and invest in relation-ships in the same way.

Boys benefit greatly from hearing their dads talk about accountability, honest dialogue, and the gift of walking in relationship with other men. Many men experience relation-ship best around shared interests or activities—golf, hunting, fishing, Bible study, music, or travel. Be sure to talk openly about those activities and experiences, and how the time serves you as a male.

Emotion

Boys need to hear men talk about failures and disappointments, hopes and dreams. They need to know the men you talk openly with when your heart is breaking or you experience fear or uncertainty.

They need to sit around the dinner table and hear the males in their lives talk about their day—the highs and lows, the wins and losses, and the emotions behind the reporting. **Boys need to see that emotions reside in the life of a man.** Pay close attention to not attaching a heroic ending to the story. Often we tell stories that involve struggle of some kind, but end with everything coming together in victory. That simply isn't real life, and it sets a boy up for believing he's doing something wrong when he comes against the hard moments of life that don't offer immediate (or any) resolution.

> **Boys benefit greatly from hearing their dads talk about accountability, honest dialogue, and the gift of walking in relationship with other men.**

Boys need to hear men talk about feeling incompetent. This world is full of stories and messages that communicate a need to navigate life without fear or uncertainty. We often frame masculinity around competence, certainty, and victory.

Then when boys bump up against the everyday experience of confusion, fear, and loss, they feel less masculine and as if their wiring is somehow faulty.

I'm working with a boy who lost his grandmother recently. She was one of the most significant adults in his life. She once brought her grandson for his appointment, and I greeted her by commenting what a pleasure it had been to know and spend time with this remarkable young man.

She grabbed my arm after we shook hands and held on tight for a moment. She looked me dead in the eyes and said, "I love this kid with my entire being. He has given me so much delight throughout his life." Her eyes filled with tears, the way it happens when we talk about kids we love. I think she could somehow tell I was firmly in his corner, another adult committed to his growing into all of who God had made him to be.

This young man spent countless hours with his grandmother in her last months and weeks. Many of those were spent with his parents in the same room. They told stories and spoke words of life to each other.

When hospice was called in, his dad climbed into the hospital bed next to her, held her, and wept uncontrollably at the thought of not being near the woman who had given him life. His son was watching every conversation and exchange. This dad was unaware of it at the time because he was grieving and simply putting one foot in front of the other.

Months later, after sitting with his son in his own grief over this loss, I reminded the dad of what he'd offered his son in walking him through loss in such an authentic way. I reminded him how few boys get to see their father modeling healthy grief. Loss is inevitable for every one of us. None of us can or will escape it.

Out of this reality we must prepare the kids we love to navigate loss. Not deny or avoid it, but to walk through it. This father offered all the ingredients we've named in this section. He validated the role his mother had played in his life, he prioritized connection for himself and his family, and he allowed his son to see that emotions reside in the life of a man. I remain grateful this boy could see all of that happen in real time.

He was also acutely aware of how his mom and dad leaned into each other throughout the loss, how his dad had friends circle around him, and how their church community served them consistently throughout the loss. It was the body of Christ being who the body of Christ was intended to be, and this young man saw it all.

Sometimes our kids sit front row to the worst this life has to offer, and sometimes the best. Even the most intentional parents will blow it at times. As long as we stop off at the third *R*, repair, when we fail our kids, there is an opportunity to model something so healthy and needed.

I've sat with countless parents who have confessed their worst moments in parenting. Moments when they lost their temper and reacted poorly. Recently, a dad I love sat in my office and confessed that he'd lost his cool when his wife had labored over a beautiful meal and new recipe, and on the third reminder for his son to come to the table, he went upstairs only to find him still gaming. He yanked the plug from the wall and yelled, "Tonight when you go to bed, I'm going to set the Xbox on FIRE!"

We laughed together at how ridiculous his words were in that moment, but then I assured him he wasn't the only parent walking the earth who wanted to burn technology to the ground. Don't we all at times?

This same father has had some of the most thoughtful, strategic conversations with his son about his growing and changing body. He has read books with him, taken him on a camping trip he turned into an initiation ceremony, and had a hundred other meaningful exchanges. He's simply living all of our reality—he's been both the best *and* worst of himself as a parent.

The hope for all of us, as mothers and fathers, is to do the work needed, to live a more wholehearted life, and to allow our kids to experience the overflow. Ultimately, we are always pointing them to a Parent who will never fail them. The only one who can offer them life, hope, joy, and peace. A peace that passes all understanding. A peace that will never make sense to the world. Peace that goes beyond our current circumstances to the eternal.

That's the greatest calling on our lives as mothers and fathers. It always has been and it always will be.

INTENTIONAL PRACTICES

1. **Ask good questions.** Questions activate problem-solving and resourcefulness. They also communicate we believe boys are competent and capable. Furthermore, they invite boys into articulating their experience more fully.

2. **One-liners.** Develop some helping statements for moments when he's most prone to anchoring or blame—statements like: "I love you too much to

argue" or "I'm sorry you're in a bad mood, but that doesn't mean you get to take it out on me." These messages keep you out of the trap of emotional tug-of-war and set the stage for resourcefulness.

3. **Blame-to-shame diagram.** Use the blame-to-shame diagram once he's done some regulation work to get himself to rational thinking and has made some needed connections. Help him fill in some declarations on both sides in order to develop some ownership statements.

4. **Support and contribution questions.** Ask him questions about where he experienced support and where he offered it, as a way of moving him outward and connecting him to purpose.

5. **Name failure.** Turn up the volume on naming moments when you, as parents, experienced failure or disappointment. Talking regularly about these experiences will normalize failure as a part of life, while also helping him avoid the trap of building an identity around competence, victory, and success.

Friends and Allies

Once upon a time I was a distance runner. No one would currently mistake me for that. Many marathons later, I've managed to put too many miles on my feet and knees, and a brisk walk around the neighborhood is my current "run."

Despite my limitations, I loved every minute of watching my kids run cross-country and track throughout their high school careers. They set personal records (PRs), became state champs, and more importantly discovered runners to be a rich community of folks.

Along the way one of my sons told me about Eliud Kipchoge, who has been described as the greatest marathoner of the modern era. He is an Olympic medalist who broke the world record for a marathon in under two hours. He was raised by a single mom in Kenya and ran two miles to school every day.

As he shattered records throughout his running career, he developed a practice that I believe every one of us could learn from, whether a runner or not. His practice is as much a life skill as a long-distance running skill. Kipchoge built a team of pacesetters. These individuals would run in front, in back, and on each side of him to help maintain a sustainable pace for whatever distance he hoped to complete. They helped him to not go out too fast in the early miles of a race, or slow down midway to a pace that would affect his desired finishing time. They helped him maintain a healthy pace by surrounding him.

I'd invite you to jump online and watch videos of his countless record-setting finishes, but more importantly to watch him run with the pacesetters. One of the more fascinating parts comes near the completion of the race when the pacesetters begin spreading out, falling back, and moving behind him to allow the desired finish to happen. It's one of the most powerful visuals of what running the race of life could look like for a person—to be surrounded by the very people who carry you through the hardest, most difficult moments of life and then celebrate your victory in completing the race.

I'd encourage you to watch the footage with your kids and allow the visual to set the stage for some great conversation. Talk about . . .

1. Who are your "pacesetters"—the friends who stay with you in the hard moments and celebrate with you in the victories?
2. Who are *you* a pacesetter for in friendship? Which friends are you supporting and cheering on in this season of life?
3. What is it like for you to fall back and celebrate your friends? When is the last time you had an

opportunity to do this? Did you feel excitement for your friend? Did you feel jealous on the inside? Did you feel a bit of both at the same time? What did you do with those feelings?

4. When was the last time you chose to thank your pacesetters—in person, through text or call, or by writing them a note?

5. Who is someone in your life who could use a pacesetter right now?

These questions could help your son (or daughter) begin to think more in this category. It's important to flesh out the third question with kids and adolescents. It's not uncommon to experience conflicting emotions as you celebrate a friend's win. Sometimes kids have difficulty knowing what to do with jealousy in those moments. Some kids feel bad about themselves for experiencing any degree of envy. At times, kids don't know what to do with those conflicting emotions, and the emotions can roadblock their capacity to show up in ways they'd hope to. Developing this idea of conflicting feelings allows more space for healthy emotional development, alongside opening up more room to be present for others.

Laugh with your happy friends when they're happy; share tears when they're down.

Romans 12:15–16 The Message

These questions also allow boys to think through what it looks like to walk out the wisdom of this passage in practical ways with their friends.

I'd invite you to talk about the pacesetters in your own life. Talk openly about the friends who run with you and move you forward when you're having a hard time. Talk about how often God provides different pacesetters in different seasons. Some of those individuals stick around from decade to decade and remain in our lives today. Some of those pacesetters were meant for a season. I had five pacesetters in high school, a handful in college, and some in young adulthood who were groomsmen in my wedding. Some of those individuals are still running the race with me today. Some of those folks are friends I love deeply but don't see or connect with that often.

Spectators and Allies

As we work with this analogy, we can also invite our kids to pay attention to the streets lined with individuals cheering on Eliud Kipchoge. Remind them that there will always be folks who cheer us on from the sidelines. They aren't pacesetters who run with us, but they play a significant role in our lives nonetheless.

I work with a large team of folks in my practice. I have close, intimate friendships with some of those individuals. Some of them I don't have the opportunity to share life with in the exact same way. It's not that I don't find them interesting or enjoyable, because I do. I'm grateful to share our work life and a commitment to an aligned mission and purpose. They've celebrated book releases, we've partnered together in fundraising events, and we talk at staff meetings. They've cheered me on from the sidelines, and I hope I've done the same for them. We've celebrated weddings and births, while also grieving losses.

The same is true for my neighbors. I have a few I share coffee and meals with on a regular basis. Others I only see at the annual block party we host on our street. There are varying degrees of relationship and involvement. It's good for our kids to understand that's a normal part of a person's relational life. Not everyone is a pacesetter and not everyone is a spectator.

Within this category it's important to talk about the types of relationships we experience online. It's possible for boys to experience a degree of connection through online gaming and social media. I know adults who share relationship with individuals they've never met in person. I, personally, don't believe it's possible to be a pacesetter for someone you've never met in person. I understand other people feel differently about this. That's okay. I'm not looking for agreement on this, only an opportunity to help boys understand there are some differences between online relationships and in-person connection.

Just as we talk with kids about how social media tends to be a highlight reel of a person's life, online relationships tend to be more one-dimensional. It's a bit like what my wife and I experienced when we dated long-distance after college. I'd travel to where she lived for long weekends, and we'd go for picnics in the mountains and romantic dates that included hours of conversation and long walks. We'd leave the weekends wishing for more time, and spend the weeks longing for the next encounter.

Twenty-five years into marriage, we look back and laugh at how likable we both were in those times. We barely knew one another and could easily present our "best selves" when we saw so little of each other and had a limited history.

We followed that season with my wife moving to Nashville, where I was living, to take a job. The weekend started with an exhausting move, limited sleep, cleaning, and trips to the grocery store—the everyday stuff of life. We traded long walks and picnics in the mountains for more of the mundane. It's not that we didn't have romantic dates and long talks, we simply folded in more normal life and came to know each other on a different level. Suffice it to say, I became much less interesting and much more ordinary.

You know you really love someone when you can eat cold pizza on the hardwood floors of an empty apartment, surrounded by boxes. You find your pacesetters when it's time to assemble a ceiling fan or an Ikea bookshelf. You find your pacesetters when you finish a hard week at work, or show up for the news of a parent with cancer.

It's difficult to experience all of relationship online when you can't do the dailiness of life together. It's not that the relationships aren't authentic or real—the interactions are simply limited. I would argue the relationship is limited as well. I believe it's easier to be a spectator than a pacesetter. The pacesetters who run alongside Eliud Kipchoge can hear him breathe. They are close enough to him to know when he's falling behind and when he's needing more support. Those things are harder to identify from a distance. The folks cheering on the side of the road can't identify those challenges in the same way. That's not to say they can't observe when Eliud may be struggling or off pace, but they don't understand it in the same way the folks running near him do.

Because they don't have the history, they don't know how to help him find his pace. They certainly can yell his name louder, or clap as he passes, but they can't offer the same kind of support those running around him can. Because of history. Because of proximity. Because of relationship.

They are allies. They've made a commitment to this man and to themselves. You don't clock in thousands of miles training for one race without sacrifice and commitment. Undoubtedly these individuals have chosen to wake before sunrise. They've run in the worst of weather, and on days when they simply didn't feel like putting on running shoes. They've sacrificed their own comfort and involvement for the sake of something outside themselves.

They've also agreed to move behind this man as the race comes to a close. When he crosses the finish line, the applause and the coverage are intended for only one person, not many. That isn't to say there won't be appreciation and acknowledgment for more than Kipchoge, but the race is "won" by one. The victory may be shared, but the medal goes around one neck.

To be an ally means you are comfortable with this arrangement. An ally is aligned with loyalty and commitment. An ally is acquainted with sacrifice and struggle. An ally is anchored to meaning and purpose.

The Disciples

It can be difficult for boys to get an accurate picture of what it looks like to be in close, intimate relationship with friends. There are multiple barriers to experiencing deep connection and community. We've already discussed how competition can serve as a barrier. Boys may be more postured to be *against* than to be *for*. Secondly, boys are socialized to be self-sufficient; having needs and needing help is a sign of weakness more than strength. Thirdly, the difficulty with articulating their experience creates internal movement rather than external expression.

Being Against + Being Self-Sufficient – External Expression = Alone

Males are more vulnerable to suffering in silence. It's no mystery why boys, adolescent males, and men lead the statistics for suicide. If you add the above equation to risk-taking behavior, it makes perfect sense. Unless we redefine the strength of emotion and the strength of connection, the outcome will remain the same.

I talk often about teaching boys what it means to live *in* the world and not *of* it. Kingdom living is upside-down living.

The last will be first.

Winning by dying.

The least are the greatest.

Power in weakness.

Blessing in suffering.

The poor become rich.

None of it makes sense in the world we live in. All of it makes sense in God's economy. Boys need to see what it looks like to live out these realities in a world that values success, independence, and competence.

I recently spent time with an amazing group of college-aged and young adult men. They are the staff at an all-boys summer camp. I spent a day talking about emotional and social development and how to best support the boys in their care. We discussed the idea of helping boys break down the meaning of upside-down kingdom living. I challenged them to talk openly with boys about their own experiences of fear and incompetence. To name the times in their lives when they felt afraid, confused, or alone. I challenged them to talk openly about their friendships and practical ways they'd experienced intimacy and connection within their relationships. I urged them to model that with each other.

We talked about allowing boys to see them relate in ways that didn't involve sarcasm, dominance, and surface conversation. We discussed how desperately boys need to see this from adult males. We talked about the mechanics of relationship and how boys need to see the practical ways a male can demonstrate support and empathy. Boys have a very clear understanding of competition and one-upping in conversation. They don't tend to have clarity about other ways of relating.

We discussed how often a boy might share news of a victory—"I scored the winning goal in my last soccer game." Rarely would this statement be met with "Congratulations" or "Dude, that's awesome." A more likely response would be "So what? I scored three goals in my last game." There's an instinctive response to one-up each other more than support.

These relational patterns can show up in moments when support is what's needed. I've witnessed boys bravely sharing about their parents' divorce or the loss of a grandparent and peers struggling to respond with empathy or support. Not because they don't genuinely care and want to be understanding, but simply because they haven't had much practice, experience, or modeling in this space. It's like being asked to play an instrument they've barely held.

Kids learn more from observation than information. When they can watch this in the adults around them, it changes the game. They then have a context and a category for empathy. The skills become more familiar and easier to execute.

Consider the Context

Think for a moment about all the places where your son spends time. From the classroom to the cul-de-sac, playdates to playing fields, youth group to the YMCA, scouts to service projects. How would you describe the culture within these spaces? Is it more a culture of kindness or cruelty? Is it more a context for competition or collaboration? What's the primary purpose of the time? How would you describe the adults in charge? How do they motivate and challenge kids?

As within a workspace or home environment, culture is everything. What are the values? What's the mission?

In my work, I've seen families make extraordinary sacrifices in seeking out contexts for growth. I've known families who downsized to a significantly smaller space and sold a vehicle to relocate to a better school district. I've known families who sacrificed long-term athletic opportunities to scale down from travel sports to a rec league that placed a higher value on character development than winning seasons. I've known parents who became volunteer coaches, PTA presidents, and youth group leaders for the sake of infusing something meaningful and needed into a context where their kids spent time.

I've known families who pulled their kids from an extracurricular experience to commit to a season of service for the sake of growth. I've known families who shut down technology for a summer and prioritized reading, outdoor activity, and volunteering. Many times these parents sacrificed peace for pushback. They were choosing character over happiness. Many times they were also creating a context for relationship. If you volunteer at the local animal shelter or build a Habitat for Humanity home, chances are good you'll intersect with other folks who have a shared vision and shared values. Signing up for your local library's summer reading program or church Cub Scout troop could lead to meeting other like-minded kids and parents.

I often talk with kids and parents about putting yourself in the way of healthy relationships. I'm not assuming this works out 100 percent of the time, but I think it certainly can open the door to meaningful connection. It's a question worth considering. It's a decision worth evaluating.

Years ago I was working with a sixteen-year-old who had experienced a series of what he called dead-end relationships. He came to the conclusion, on his own, that he was looking in all the wrong places. He reported, "I've got a better chance of meeting a great girl at Young Life than I do at a party with marijuana." I told him he had a sound argument. This kid was wisely figuring out how to put himself in the way of healthier relationships. He was making connections that some of his "dead-end relationships" came from meeting people connected to unhealthy habits in destructive places.

We moved from place and time to qualities and values. We began talking about what he'd learned from past relationships. Relationships are great teachers. We can learn something of value even from the difficult ones. We learn more about what we want in future relationships when we take the time to consider what we've learned from past relationships. What worked and didn't work? What did we offer to the relationship that was of value? Where do we need to grow? What qualities did the other person contribute that we'd want or want to avoid?

It's good to get feedback from outside sources. I challenge boys to ask their best friend, parents, a close friend who is a girl, and another trusted adult to weigh in on what they observed about the relationship. Many times we are simply too close to the relationship to be objective, but others can reflect something valuable from a different angle. It takes courage, humility, and wisdom to receive feedback, particularly when the feedback may be hard to hear.

But the feedback allows us to more strategically put ourselves in the way of healthier relationships. It allows us to formulate better responses to questions about friendships and dating relationships like

Who are people that move me in a better direction?
What are the qualities of people who help me be a better version of myself?
What am I looking for in a friend or girlfriend?
What is my definition of a *quality* relationship?
How am I putting myself in the way of healthy relationships?

Obviously a boy's responses to these kinds of questions will be limited by age, maturity, and experience. His capacity for thinking backward and forward becomes more developed over time. If he doesn't develop reflective skills like we discussed in an earlier chapter, he's more vulnerable to living out that classic definition of insanity—doing the same thing over and over expecting a different result.

Quality over Quantity

The longer I work with boys, the more I am convinced that it only takes a few. Let me explain. If a boy can find one or two good friends who are moving in the same direction, that's all it takes. If he graduates from high school with six or seven great friends, that's amazing, but it isn't necessary. He may have a large circle of relationships, but it's unlikely he will have deep, meaningful connection with three dozen people. It's not only unlikely, it's somewhat impossible. He can't go deep with that many people. He can have a range of connections, but he needs only a couple of allies. He can have a number of spectators, but he needs only a few loyal pacesetters. Keep moving him back to the questions in this chapter that allow him to evaluate and re-evaluate his relationships.

This evaluation will serve him well as he graduates and begins living on his own for the first time. At that point, the hope is that he can do more of this evaluation on his own. We want him to have developed skills in identifying healthy relationships—male and female—that offer the needed support, connection, and community we all need as relationally driven people.

Boys can benefit from reading about the friendship between David and Jonathan in 1 Samuel 18. Talk about what it means to be "knit to the soul" of someone. This passage describes an intimate connection between two friends. It speaks to a fierce loyalty that weathers many seasons within a relationship.

This same intimacy and loyalty are woven throughout the relationship between Christ and his disciples. Help boys evaluate how Christ interacted with these men. How they walked together, lived in close proximity, and invested deeply in one another. Help them make connections around how different these interactions are from how most adult males interact. I believe it's helpful for boys to see the fruit of men having intimate connection, and how it yielded a healthy sense of community between Jesus and his disciples versus the statistics shared early in the book about men who struggle to reach out for help and live in isolation.

INTENTIONAL PRACTICES

1. **Define** *pacesetter*. Spend time defining what it means to be a pacesetter for others and to have them in your own life. Make a list of qualities that make a good pacesetter. Make a list of roles a pacesetter performs.

2. **Identify pacesetters.** Help boys identify the supportive friends who help them stay on pace. Ask if they can name who those folks are in your life and give concrete examples of how your pacesetters have served you in different seasons.

3. **Give thanks.** Move from definition and identification into gratitude. Write notes together thanking the friends who've offered needed support and played a vital role in your lives. Boys benefit from seeing their parents acknowledging the value of friendships.

4. **Compare and contrast.** Study examples throughout Scripture of how different men operate in friendship. Compare those examples to how most men function

in relationship and how the world defines relationship between males.

5. **Upside-down connections.** Spend time helping boys make needed connections around upside-down kingdom living. Discuss what it feels like to serve and give to others.

Models and Mentors

I recently sat with a dad in his midforties. He's a pastor and is contemplating his future. While talking about his kids, he commented he worried about how they perceived the work he did in light of how burned-out he was. He voiced concern that not only would it impact how his boys saw a man's vocational life, but more importantly how it might impact them spiritually because he worked in vocational ministry.

His wife challenged him to consider meeting with some pastors in their sixties who had been in vocational ministry for decades and were still in happy marriages and engaged with their adult children. He sat and thought for a long period of time and realized he couldn't identify a single man. He was heartbroken by this reality. He knew plenty of pastors who'd left the ministry and gone into other fields. He knew several who'd lost their marriage, and countless who had fractured relationships with their adult children or no relationship at all.

He was in no way saying the pastor his wife described didn't exist—he simply realized how uncommon it is for those relationships and for passion for pastoral ministry to still be intact. He was burdened not to be in close proximity to another man who'd walked the same path and was farther down the road. We processed what it felt like to stumble into this reality, and how much he wanted to be able to offer something different to his own children.

We all need models and mentors. It's important to have other parents around us who are walking out the same seasons we're in. Parents who understand the sleep deprivation of having a newborn, the tantrums of a toddler, or the eye rolling of a teenager. Parents who are in the thick of it *with* us and understand the daily challenges we are facing.

We also need parents who've traveled *ahead* of us and can cast a vision for what's to come. One of my dearest friends is a decade ahead of me. My three children are currently in college. His three are all married adults. I'm on the front side of being an empty nester. He is a beloved grandfather. I need his wisdom and experience. He has made it available to me in every season of my kids' lives. From teething to dating, from the first day of kindergarten to the first day of college, and everything in between. He has fielded over a thousand questions in our thirty-year friendship, and he reminds me often that you never stop being a parent. Just because your kids move out and become adults who are parents themselves, you never stop worrying or wondering how they are. You still lose sleep when they struggle, and you still want them to come home.

My wise friend has challenged me to trust and listen more, to react and regret less, and to walk out the wisdom of the Serenity Prayer in my journey as a parent. One of my hopes is that through transformative relationships like this, I'm growing and changing. I recently heard a dad say he hoped his kids would one day say he was someone who was aware of his failures and transformed over time. He hoped his kids could identify the difference between who he was when they were young and who he became over the decades they knew him. He hoped they would see what Jesus did to him, through prayer and community, and that it would give them hope for who they could become in Christ.

I talk often about the time I spend in the company of wise friends. I hope my kids could identify my three closest friends and how their lives have shaped my own. How these friends have mentored me into being a man, a husband, and a father.

I believe they've watched how their grandfather, my father, has shaped me. I am still learning from watching his example. We all need people who've walked ahead of us. We need multigenerational community. In our neighborhoods, churches, and families. I worry this is happening less than ever. I worry how many churches across the country are led by individuals in their late twenties and early thirties. Let me be clear in saying I believe those individuals have something extraordinary to offer, but they also have much to learn.

I'm incredibly grateful to be pastored by two men in their sixties and seventies. I'm thankful my boss is in her early seventies and my dad is in his late seventies. I have neighbors and friends who are five, ten, and twenty years ahead of me. I'm grateful to be surrounded by so much wisdom and lived experience. Proverbs reminds us of the importance of this.

> Listen, friends, to some fatherly advice;
> sit up and take notice so you'll know how to live.
> I'm giving you good counsel;
> don't let it go in one ear and out the other.

When I was a boy at my father's knee,
the pride and joy of my mother,
He would sit me down and drill me:
"Take this to heart. Do what I tell you—live!
Sell everything and buy Wisdom! Forage for
  Understanding!
Don't forget one word! Don't deviate an inch!
Never walk away from Wisdom—she guards your life;
love her—she keeps her eye on you.
Above all and before all, do this: Get Wisdom!
Write this at the top of your list: Get Understanding!
Throw your arms around her—believe me, you
  won't regret it;
never let her go—she'll make your life glorious.
She'll garland your life with grace,
she'll festoon your days with beauty."
Dear friend, take my advice;
it will add years to your life.
I'm writing out clear directions to Wisdom Way,
I'm drawing a map to Righteous Road.
I don't want you ending up in blind alleys,
or wasting time making wrong turns.
Hold tight to good advice; don't relax your grip.
Guard it well—your life is at stake!

Proverbs 4:1–13 The Message

A Collective

Wisdom comes from lived experience. Wisdom also comes from surrounding yourself with folks who outpace you. I believe much of the wisdom I've collected was birthed out of marrying out of my league, befriending folks who outrun me, and working alongside a team that outperforms me. I'm simply surrounded by people who are smarter, stronger, wiser, and more talented than I am, and it has served me beautifully. I could spend a lot of time swimming in envy and jealousy, but I'd prefer to just learn and let their collective talents spill out onto me.

> In the multitude of counselors there is safety.
>
> Proverbs 11:14 NKJV

As the famous saying goes, we are the average of the five people we spend the most time with. This would be a great conversation to have with your son throughout his development. Ask him to identify the five people he spends the most time with, and to reflect on their influence (good or bad). Ask him to identify the five people you spend the most time with. See if he's on target or not in his assessment. Then speak to the influence of your top five and something unique you've learned or are learning from each of them.

Wisdom comes from surrounding yourself with folks who outpace you.

I mentioned earlier that one of my grandfathers was a builder. He fought in World War II, and the flag from his funeral is framed in my office. I also have a collection of his antique tools that I've placed throughout my home and in my office. From him, I learned about bravery and building.

My other grandfather loved to fish. I have a tackle box he gave me as a boy. It has my name on it and is the only thing I own with his handwriting. From him, I learned about patience and endurance.

My father-in-law was one of the most gracious, warm, engaging men I've had the pleasure of knowing. He lived the words of never meeting a stranger. Watching him over the decades taught me the value of engaging others and helping people feel seen and known.

My own father is one of the most kindhearted men I could have hoped to spend a lifetime with. He was a passionate educator throughout my life, and even more passionate about his faith. From him, I developed a love of learning, the strength of curiosity, and evidence of what it looks like to walk with God for seven decades.

Those are just my fathers and grandfathers. I could easily list the impact of my wife, my boss, my colleagues, my pastor, and my dearest friends. Being in close proximity to these people has profoundly shaped who I am and has been a wellspring of wisdom and lived experience.

Just as I've been positively influenced by these individuals, boys can be negatively shaped by the people in their lives. I sit with parents on a weekly basis who have concerns about their sons' friends or girlfriends. We can't choose our kids' friends, but we can help them make connections. I've known parents who tried to force a breakup with a girlfriend and created a Romeo-and-Juliet type of situation.

While we can't choose those relationships, we certainly have the power to influence the kind of time they spend with them while they're under eighteen. I challenge parents who have concerns over the lack of supervision or oversight at another family's home to simply say to their sons, "I don't know the parents well enough for you to spend time there, but you are welcome to have your friend over to our house." Or, "I suspect we may have different rules or ideas about what's okay and what's not, so I'm agreeing to you hanging out here but not there." We aren't limiting the opportunity to have relationship, but we are creating a safer context for time together.

Many boys are angered by this response and will refuse the time. My experience is they typically give in over time if the relationship means enough to them, or it works itself out. Many boys are aware of the friends who'd violate the boundaries in their own home and simply don't want to deal with the hassle and consequences of what that would mean for them.

You can treat a dating relationship the same way. Keep welcoming her into your home if you have concerns about how they will spend the time together and then have ownership over the oversight and supervision. I call this a "no/yes" response. You are saying no to the location and yes to the relationship. The yes allows you to get to know the friend or girlfriend and discern more about the relationship.

It's important to note that some boys will find their way to dangerous and destructive relationships. I've consulted with parents of young boys who discover inappropriate touch has taken place with a peer, and it becomes necessary to draw strong boundaries around that relationship and seek needed support. I've worked with adolescent boys who stopped being boyfriends and ended up as crisis counselors for adolescent girls. She was using the relationship as a hostage crisis, threatening self-harm and requiring him to be her lifeline. I've known boys who have friends that won't respect the boundaries of their home and bring illegal substances on the premises. At any point your son is in the way of harm, it's not only appropriate but necessary to intervene. When harm is in the equation, it's no longer a "no/yes" but a "no/no" with the priority being on his safety. It's vital to distinguish between relationships that have a negative bent to them and those that are unsafe.

Other Voices

In the same way we are thinking intentionally about the peer influences in our sons' lives, we want to think strategically about the adult voices as well. It's common that other adults can get away with speaking into his life in a unique way. It's part of why many boys perform consistently for teachers and coaches while pushing hard against parents.

I remind parents of adolescents that it's common our voices as parents will get softer and the voices of his peers and other adults get louder. Think about teachers, coaches, youth pastors, and friends' parents who had a strong presence in your own adolescence. Consider professors, campus ministers, and other adults who influenced you throughout the college years.

When our voice gets softer, it's tempting to talk *more* and talk *louder*. Neither approach is effective. The better response is to put your son in the way of other healthy adult voices. Think strategically about the leagues where your son will participate in sports and the kinds of coaches those leagues attract. When exploring churches, spend time with the adults who run the children's and youth ministries. If it seems difficult to find these trusted adult voices, consider hiring them. Yes, you read that correctly.

I worked with parents years ago whose son had become resistant to youth group, and it had become a battle for the family that wasn't worth fighting. This young man played one sport that ran for eight weeks. The other ten months of the year, he was void of other adult voices except for some great teachers who only saw him an hour a day during the school year. His parents reached out to a campus minister friend at a local college and asked for the names of some trusted college-aged boys who might want to earn some extra money. They interviewed three boys and hired one with a group of six parents to form a small group for their sons. They ended up meeting together for three years of high school and formed foundational relationships. This college-aged young man benefited from mentoring (and some extra cash), and this group of adolescent boys benefited from the investment of a really cool college kid who was walking with Christ a season beyond them.

I worked with a single mom who joined forces with four other single moms to hire a young married man at their church to lead a book club for their fifth graders. The moms rotated hosting the club in their homes and prepared food, and the boys benefited from spending time in the company of a healthy adult male who was interested and invested in each of them. He was modeling what it looked like for males to become readers and learners, to have thoughtful conversation, and to listen without judgement. There were layers of social and emotional benefit through the simplicity of this experience for these young boys, all of whom were growing up without fathers.

I know another family who hired a great college kid to form a church league basketball team for their sons. Basketball was simply the vehicle for bringing these guys together. Practice turned into practice plus burgers. Games led to Saturday hangs. The boys finished their last season by ordering vintage uniforms online. They dressed for every game like players straight out of the 1950s. The photos were priceless. The mentoring that took place was the real victory of this experience.

Be as strategic, creative, and prayerful as you can in ushering in other voices throughout your son's development. His capacity to hear from these voices is extraordinary. Let's capitalize on this reality.

Media Voices

As captivated as boys are with all things technology and media, let's be strategic in capitalizing on it as well. This will take some guidance and exposure. Left to their own devices (pun intended), boys may not find their way to the most constructive voices. Whether it's music or YouTube, sadly many boys gravitate toward the lowest common denominator. It grieves me that with all the great music out there, boys can tend to huddle around a small handful of artists who primarily use profanity, elevate drug culture, and demoralize women in their lyrics. Unfortunately, these can be the same ingredients with those they follow on YouTube and TikTok. Use this fascination as an opportunity to develop critical thinking, and put good boundaries in place on their devices with explicit content.

Sometimes boys simply need more exposure to other options. Thankfully there are still great voices on social media using that platform for good. There are strong voices in the athletic and entertainment space who aren't using those same negative ingredients to produce content.

The same goes for movies and television shows. There's plenty of dark content out there, alongside some great storytelling that can be a vehicle for developing critical thinking alongside healthy mentoring. Boys can be mentored through fictional characters. As you watch shows and movies together as a family, dissect the characters and identify areas of strength and weakness. Highlight characters who have qualities that resonate with you—a quality you embody or one you hope to acquire. Do this with books and media. Allow these voices to be tools for growth and development.

42 is an incredible movie that well illustrates how we are enculturated into an understanding of something. The movie is a beautiful portrayal of the life of Jackie Robinson, who became the first African American to play in major league baseball. There's a heartbreaking scene where a young boy is seated in the stands next to his father. As Jackie steps onto the field, his father and the crowd begin shouting horrific racist statements. The young boy is noticeably troubled. He sits with the discomfort and then tragically begins chanting the same racist declarations as his father. It's a reminder of how mentoring works. How powerful a force it can be for good or bad. It's a reminder that racism is taught not born.

The scene could be a powerful teaching tool on so many levels for boys. Have boys identify characters with strength and integrity in the movie. Have them identify individuals with these same qualities in their own life. Ask boys about their own encounters with racism. Use this important story to help boys make needed connections.

A New Framework

When I was growing up, every athletic experience ended with a handshake or a high five. I have a thousand memories of completing a game or match and walking to the center of the court to shake hands or high five the opposing team. My coach would always shake hands with the opposing coach.

No matter how the game went down, regardless of who won or lost, everyone involved would shake hands or high five at the end. This started in elementary school and went all the way through high school. This felt like an important way to end a competition—a commitment to civility and respect. The acknowledgment that it was just a game. I certainly remember times of not wanting to go through the motions of congratulating a team that had defeated mine. I'm grateful I was required to do so anyway. I think it was a useful practice on so many levels.

I don't see that practice as often anymore. I don't see this demonstration of civility and respect as much in youth sports today. In fact, I've seen some of the worst of human behavior happen on an athletic court or field. And when I say worst behavior, it wasn't usually from the young players, but from the grown-ups.

I once worked with a divorced family, and the father was suspended from attending his son's football games. The son was in fifth grade at the time. His dad would scream profanity from the stands until a referee came to the side of the field and threatened to have him leave. He'd then cuss out the referee until the head of school approached him with a warning. After the third warning, he received a letter from the board of trustees at his son's private school informing him he could no longer attend school-sponsored athletic events.

I've heard countless boys tell stories of their coaches being dragged off the field or court during a game and what it was like to watch that happen. Recently I saw a post online from the West Marin Little League with "Reminders from your Child." It read,

I'm a kid
It's just a game
My coach is a volunteer
The officials are human
NO college scholarships will be handed out today

It's disappointing to think we've reached a point where we need visual reminders for the grown-ups to allow kids to have a full and beneficial experience in youth sports. It's heartbreaking to know this kind of modeling is happening across the country. Kids learn more from observation than information. They desperately need to see good modeling. They need adults who model winning and losing. They need grown-ups who are implementing the kinds of healthy coping skills we've been talking about throughout this book. On and off the field, and in the everyday moments of life.

Sadly many boys are witnessing men who are *in* pain and *causing* pain. Often a boy lacks skills simply because he hasn't seen enough evidence of something—a failure of imagination. I once heard it said that discomfort is the price of admission to a meaningful life. Boys simply need to see the grown-ups around them modeling how to navigate the discomfort of life this side of heaven.

INTENTIONAL PRACTICES

1. **Top-five influences.** Ask your son to identify the five people he spends the most time with. Who are the five outside of family?

2. **Identify your village.** It really does take a village to raise a child. Make a list of the folks in your village in this particular season. Who are the other trusted adult voices in your son's life (teachers, coaches, extended family, other parents, youth pastors, Scout masters, etc.)?

3. **Media voices.** Ask your son to list the voices in media he spends the most time with (artists, musicians, professional athletes, entertainers, influencers, etc.). Ask what drew him to their message and what he believes each of them stands for.

4. **Books and movies.** Make a list of books to read and movies to watch that invite boys to experience healthy modeling and mentoring through characters. Check out @raisingboysandgirls on Instagram for a list of great books and movies for kids from toddlers to teens that include great stories and characters to study. Common Sense Media also has lists of great movies and shows to watch with kids based on ages and stages of life.

5. **Pay it forward.** It's not only important to identify folks who've been great mentors, but to think about mentoring others. Ask your son, whatever his age, to identify one person he believes he can influence for good. Have him share a memory of a time when he served as a mentor to someone in his path.

8

Upward and Outward

By now, you've likely discovered my appreciation for cross-country running. I love the sport for a thousand reasons. It teaches endurance and persistence. You are a part of a team and also setting individual goals. It allows for endless hours in nature, and it is, in my mind, a great metaphor for life. Life is not a sprint, it's a marathon. It's a long, enduring run, full of highs and lows, losses and victories.

All three of my kids ran cross-country during high school. My daughter came home junior year after a brutal practice and shared an amazing insight from her coach. On this particular day they were training on hills, the heat was suffocating, and everyone was running low on endurance. Her coach challenged the team with a practice for the worst moments of the uphill climb. *When your mind is locked into the pain and anguish of the uphill climb, and it's hard to imagine pushing through, turn your attention outward. Start cheering for a teammate.*

I loved her words. I loved this challenge. She wasn't pretending this would take away the discomfort, it would simply redirect it into some kind of purpose.

Her coach knew the wisdom of attention. We can't give 100 percent of our attention to the discomfort if we're turning it toward cheering on a friend. I believe this outward movement is not only a strategy for running, but wisdom for life. I believe it's within our calling as believers to love God and love others. We want to always be turning our attention upward and outward.

This practice beckons back to the definition of resourcefulness we discussed early on in this book—taking the emotion to something constructive. As we consider this, it's of great importance to dissect the meaning. On the surface, this could look like avoidance or denial. Pretending the discomfort isn't there and acting accordingly.

That's not at all what my daughter's coach was communicating and not what I'm recommending. The first third of this book is devoted to the strength of emotion. Understanding my own and leaning into the emotions of others. Dr. Susan David, a Harvard Medical School psychologist, has done extensive research on emotional agility, or the skills of being healthy with self and others. Dr. David believes our emotions signpost the things we care about and the things we need.[1] As we've already discussed, they aren't good or bad—they are simply signaling to us a need.

Once we acknowledge the need, then we can attend to it. Emotional agility means I use my feelings to guide me in my values. My core value as a person of faith is to move upward and outward, to love God and others. This value is what guided my daughter's coach to recommend moving the discomfort toward purpose.

This coach wisely knew the satisfaction that would come from championing teammates in the hardest parts of the run. The satisfaction we experience in others-centered living has been biologically and neurologically proven. Having purpose and offering support have a profound impact on our well-being. Research has proven where this can lower levels of the stress hormone cortisol and release more of the feel good chemicals.

For example, one study found that middle school students who mentored younger students, helping them with their study habits, spent more time on their own homework. Finding meaning, discovering purpose, and serving others impacts physical and emotional well-being on many levels.[2]

> Having purpose and offering support profoundly impact our well-being.

If we stack this data next to the researched benefits of having a spiritual life—better health outcomes, less anxiety and depression, improved coping skills, and greater longevity, to name a few—we confirm the benefits of upward and outward movement.[3] As with everything we've discussed, it starts with our own experience so that we can model this consistently for the boys we love, and then help them develop more in this area.

Outward Emotionally

As we think about helping boys move outward emotionally, it could be helpful to use a diagram in explaining this concept to them and helping us understand it better ourselves.

Feelings   ⟵————⟶   Emotional Response

We have an experience, and within that we have feelings about what's happening. We take in those feelings (inward movement) and have an emotional response (outward movement). Remember, feelings are just feelings. They aren't good or bad, right or wrong. They are simply signaling us in some way. What we do with those feelings could be good or bad, right or wrong, healthy or unhealthy. If we can use our Top Five List, there's a great chance the emotional response will be more constructive and helpful. If we release the physicality of the emotion, intensity doesn't build up inside of us. If we do some deep breathing to move the blood flow back to our prefrontal cortex, we can think rationally. We can talk about what's happening rather than saying, "I don't know." All of this is healthy outward movement.

If we open up rather than shutting down, we set the stage for a constructive emotional response. When boys bottle things up, refuse to go to the Space, or won't test-drive the Top Five List, they are simply creating a buildup of inward movement. It's like a volcano, and when there's a buildup of too much hot lava inside, it's going to erupt.

Use that analogy of a volcano. You may even want to include it on the diagram. It may be a useful teaching tool for helping boys make connections around inward and outward movement. Another concrete tool can be blowing up a balloon. Pause between breaths and name difficult circumstances that would generate strong feelings. Continue blowing until the balloon is about to pop. Ask boys what they believe will happen if the buildup continues.

Talk with boys about how much healthy outward movement happens outdoors. Obviously many of the Top Five List ideas may involve something outside. Beyond that, discuss all the health benefits of being in nature. Being in nature can "lower blood pressure and stress hormone levels, reduce nervous system arousal, enhance immune system function, increase self-esteem, reduce anxiety, and improve mood."[4]

When I sit with parents in a first appointment, I often ask them to talk about when their son is at his best. When he is the most content, the happiest, the most himself. The two most common answers I hear are during one-on-one time and when he's outside. I believe most boys are capable of being their best selves when playing outdoors, whether it's imaginative play, explorative play, or athletic play. When he's moving, exploring, and experiencing nature, it brings out the best in him.

Think about how the opposite is also true. The majority of conflict I hear parents describe centers around technology. Battles erupt over turning off a device, setting limits, respecting limits, or violating limits. Limiting screen time will always be a battle worth fighting when it comes to boys. They desperately need limits in this area, and they always need the benefit of time outdoors.

When you take hikes as a family, ride bikes, canoe, kayak, climb, camp, or simply walk around the block with your family dog, talk about how different you feel at the close of that time. I've never been emotionally charged, taken a walk, and then felt worse. I always feel better. More settled. More regulated. More integrated.

Some of the richest conversations with my kids have happened while walking in our neighborhood. I've *purposefully* had some of the hardest conversations with them while walking. Keep going back to how well side-by-side conversations work compared to eye-to-eye. All of these ideas fit within this category of outward movement.

Outward Relationally

We have a park next to our office, and there's a loop around the park that's ideal for walking the therapy dogs we use in our practice. I've had some rich conversations with boys walking that loop. I'm convinced they are unaware how often they disclose things they may not have intended to share as openly on those walks. The movement is settling and creates more space for good conversation.

Feelings ⟵⟶ Opening Up

I think it's important for boys to understand the statistics that men are more reluctant to openly discuss their health (physical or mental health). The tendency to isolate versus reach out is great in males, and the earlier we educate boys on this inward movement, the better. The same diagram could be helpful in thinking strategically about the outward movement toward relationships. Go back to the brainstorming we did on identifying allies in previous chapters.

One practice I often recommend to parents is to purchase a journal and write back and forth with their son. You can even use some of the journaling prompts recommended for him in earlier chapters as a jumping off point to begin this practice, where you both answer the same question or finish the same sentence.

I've encouraged parents of young boys to try a concrete experiment to help their sons make connections regarding the importance of this outward relational movement. I'll have them pack a backpack full of books. Make sure the backpack is heavy. Have your son put on the backpack and ask him what it feels like to carry that much weight around.

Use some conversation starters or questions, and with each answer remove one book. Have boys try the backpack on at different intervals to highlight the benefits of a little sharing, a lot of sharing, and unloading everything you are carrying. Talk with boys about the backpack experiment being an example of carrying around all your feelings or thoughts alone, and the difference it makes to unload those with a trusted person in your life. Discuss how our hearts get tired when we bottle up all of our feelings. Our brains get tired when we carry around all those thoughts without releasing them in a safe relationship.

I'd also recommend, when the backpack is still somewhat full, having him turn it around and wear it on the front. Use that as an illustration for how much harder it is to get close to people when we are carrying all that "extra baggage." It not only weighs us down, it stands in the way of our connections and relationships. Basically it gets in the way on so many levels.

On that note of thoughts and feelings, it's worth mentioning that over time emotions have become gendered. We often talk with girls about how they *feel*, and with boys about what they *did*. In doing so, we are not only missing an opportunity for boys to develop an emotional vocabulary, but in some ways communicating they don't have emotions. It's okay to ask him questions about how he spent the day and what he did, but be sure to ask about how he felt about the events as well. Use the feelings chart to turn fill-in-the-blank into multiple choice. Doing so will not only strengthen the emotional muscles, but build familiarity in sharing about his internal world within safe relationships.

I once spoke to a group of professional men who were part of a forum. These men were all executives and heads of corporations or companies. They'd met through membership in a national organization and committed to meeting together on a monthly basis. These men clearly faced unique challenges in managing organizations and all the personal and professional challenges that would come with being the person at the top.

I thought their commitment to meeting together was admirable, wise, and one of the best investments they could make in their work, marriages, and parenting.

They began every meeting by talking openly about their marriages and parenting. They would identify struggles they were facing and practices they were inhabiting. They shared books, podcasts, counselor referrals, and a range of other resources in an effort to support each other in sustaining those priority relationships. They purposefully set aside a designated amount of time specific to this part of their forum meetings. It came first as a way of communicating its priority and making sure it was never bumped from the agenda.

Then and only then would they move into talking about the challenges they were facing and the growth they were experiencing in the workplace.

The forum meetings often included education. They asked me to come and speak about parenting, and more specifically about their role as fathers. I began my talk by affirming what they were doing and reminding them how rare the community they'd built was among men in this world. I went on to say their model was something men's groups in churches could really learn from.

Not only were they prioritizing their personal lives above their professional lives, but they were prioritizing and practicing sharing on an honest level what they were facing as husbands and fathers. As if that weren't significant enough, I highlighted the fact that bringing me in to speak was evidence of a desire to grow and learn. Something every one of us should continue throughout development. We shouldn't stop being students simply because we finish our formal schooling experience. There is always more to learn. The outward relational movement we are highlighting is one of the most extraordinary contexts for growth.

Outward Spiritually

These wise men were modeling something else I wish every boy could see. By meeting and sharing together, they were confirming their need to be together. These men were pushing against the statistics about men not reaching out for help. Despite being highly successful vocationally and, for most of them, at the top of their game, they were quick to acknowledge their need for each other. Few men are comfortable acknowledging this need. I've long experienced that some of the healthiest parents I work with are those in recovery. When you've worked the Twelve Steps, you understand the importance of identifying your need for God and others. It's foundational to recovery work.

You have come to a place of admitting you are powerless and the only way forward is in asking for help. That's the beauty of attending recovery meetings. It's the ongoing, consistent practice of coming together in safe community and acknowledging your need.

Though Scripture is incredibly clear in God asking us to come to him when we are weary and burdened, helpless and in need, we struggle with doing so as males. The invitation is clear, but the practice is difficult. Until we learn to pray with honesty, speak with honesty, and act with honesty, we will continue to rely on our own strength. Relying on our own strength and posturing as competent will always serve as a barrier to our need for Jesus. We simply cannot be independent and dependent at the same time.

It seems important to acknowledge how contradictory this way of being in the world is to the common phrase "Man up!" I think about how often males speak and hear those words. If you really think about it, the message there is to stop feeling, start doing, and take care of things on your own. The message burdens males with a need to carry everything on their own and not need help. Not help from God or help from others. I believe the opposite to be true. We are fully masculine when we feel deeply, grieve deeply, and connect with our longings. We are our best selves when we acknowledge our need for God and others. I'd encourage you to dissect the phrase "Man up!" on your own and with the boys in your care. Talk about what it most often means and how harmful the message is and how contradictory to the wisdom of Scripture. Discuss the likelihood that phrase has impacted the scary statistics regarding men's well-being. Use this as a jumping off point for delving into upward and outward living.

At my home church in Nashville, we end every service with a benediction. Our pastor explains the benediction as a blessing. He speaks Scripture over us as a blessing before we go back out into the world. He asks that we hold our palms up when we receive the benediction. Something about this posture is meant to remind us of our need for the blessing. It's also meant to remind us of what we bring to the spiritual equation. I bring nothing and Jesus brings everything. I need everything he has for me, and standing with my palms open is a reminder of that each week.

I've learned I need the reminder more than once a week. Therefore, I pray each morning with my palms open. Sitting in this position has anchored me daily to this reminder. I've come to notice that when my palms are open, my head seems to be facing upward more than in a bowed position. That may seem trivial to you, but for me it's important.

As a man, I've come to realize how much time I spend worrying over things in a way that assumes they are solely in my control. Despite everything I know to be true, and everything I believe about who God is and who I am in him, I can live less like a son of the King and more like an abandoned orphan. I operate as if I'm solely responsible for providing for my family, and I have to do it on my own.

Looking upward reminds me that I have an inheritance. It also reminds me that I have a calling on my life. As my friends Jay and Katherine Wolf spoke over their sons, "God made you to do the hard thing in the good story He's writing for your life."[5]

God made me to do hard things in the good story. I cannot do those hard things apart from his power and strength. I can't look outward effectively unless I first look upward.

I believe every boy needs those words spoken over him. He needs to know he is capable of hard things and he was made for good work. Purpose and meaning are hardwired into who we are as human beings.

I believe males are at their very best when they are intersecting with purpose. Boys tap into who they were made to be and a healthy sense of power and strength when they encounter purpose.

The boys I've seen struggle the most in twenty-five years of doing this work are boys void of purpose. Even boys who have access to incredible resources. If they are lacking in purpose, they can get lost.

> **Your son needs to know that he is capable of hard things and was made for good work.**

I believe it's why Mister Rogers's mother challenged him to look for the helpers when he saw scary things on the news. It anchored him not only to a sense of hope, but also to meaning and purpose. He could point at people doing hard things in the good story. And seeing that somehow calls a person to meaning and purpose.

When we believe we can help someone, we help ourselves. When boys can move outward with purpose, they tap into more of who they were made to be. It could be tutoring a classmate in a subject he's skilled in or helping coach a younger sibling's soccer team. Taking cookies to an elderly neighbor or making a card for a relative who is sick. Volunteering at a local animal shelter or building a Habitat house. Having a part-time job or interning at a nonprofit. All of these opportunities connect him to the healthy outward movement toward purpose.

He's not only looking for the helpers, he is becoming one. Watch for where you can help him make connections. Frederick Buechner wrote, "The place God calls you to is the place where your deep gladness and the world's deep hunger meet."[6] Boys need support in discerning that place. Our emotions can help signpost us to this place.

I believe anger is foundational to moral courage. If you feel anger as you watch the news, allow that emotion to move you toward justice and mercy in this world. It's signaling you to where you value equity in the world. When we feel anger, we are more likely to use our voice against the wrongs of this world. How could you take steps toward that? How could you help your son tap in to where his values are being exposed through his emotions?

Isn't that a different way to see and experience anger?

And what about sadness? I lost my mother to cancer several years ago, and I've felt overwhelming amounts of sadness in the wake of that loss. The sadness reminds me she was one of the most important people in my world and cues me to remember her aloud and let those feelings rise to the surface. Sadness is part of the grief process. Stopping the sadness would roadblock the grief process. That process is vital to my healing.

Losing my mother has made me a different kind of friend as I walk with others who are losing a parent. I'm more attuned, more compassionate than I've ever been. It has moved me into inviting others to share memories and stories. It has carved out a deeper place of empathy in me and allowed me to move into more pain and loss with people who are suffering.

Richard Rohr said, "If we do not transform our pain, we will most assuredly transmit it."[7] Or as the famous saying goes, hurt people hurt people. According to the statistics shared early in this book, males are the most vulnerable to hurting people with their own hurt. I believe males are *causing* so much pain through addiction, infidelity, suicide, and other harming behaviors, primarily because they are *in* pain. Pain that could be alleviated through outward and upward movement. Boys need to know their pain can be transformed into something. They need to know they can take the emotion to something constructive. They can't do that unless they know what the emotion is and learn to pay attention to it and move toward something useful. They need to see evidence in the adults around them of how to move the emotion outward and upward.

> **Boys need to know their pain can be transformed into something constructive.**

Emotions signpost the things we care about and need. Emotions aren't to be feared but understood. They aren't to be avoided but accepted. They are part of how God made us. They are one of the ways he allows us to connect with our need for him and others. Our job is to identify the balance of inward and outward movement. The outward movement is what connects us more to purpose and meaning in this world. It's what allows us to do hard things in the good story, and to offer hope to a hurting world.

> May the God of hope fill you with all joy and peace in believing, so that by the power of the Holy Spirit you may abound in hope.
>
> Romans 15:13 ESV

INTENTIONAL PRACTICES

1. **Use the diagrams.** Use the diagrams in this chapter to help boys make some connections between inward and outward movement. Have them give examples of each as a way of gauging their understanding of the concepts. You can share a personal example as well.

2. **Outward contexts.** Identify three contexts for movement and conversation (hiking, bike riding, walking the dog, etc.) that would invite space for better conversation.

3. **Journaling.** Consider back-and-forth journaling with questions or prompts as a way to help him articulate some things that may be harder to access. You can do this through pictures with boys who are too young to write.

4. **The backpack experiment.** Follow the instructions for the stages of the backpack experiment to help boys have a concrete experience of what carrying thoughts, emotions, and experiences feels like *and* how it serves as a barrier in relationships.

5. **Finding purpose.** Read the Buechner quote to him and talk about what it means. Help him begin to make connections to how God will place particular burdens and needs inside of him as a way of leading him to his calling. Help him identify one of those now and how he could turn that need into purpose. Share a personal example from your own life through work, volunteering, or service.

Habits and Practices

As school winds down each year, I talk with boys and parents about the summer. I believe summer offers unique space for boys to grow and develop outside the restraints of the academic calendar. There are endless opportunities available for boys of all ages. Everything from summer camp to family vacations. Part-time jobs to volunteer opportunities. Developing new skills to enhancing old ones. Summer reading to screen-free sabbaths. Outdoor adventures to indoor internships. It's fun to dream with families about using those months in thoughtful, intentional ways.

I often ask boys what kind of summer they hope to have. On occasion I'll hear about learning a new skill, getting a part-time job, setting a summer goal, or starting a new business. Often, I get the exact same answer . . .

I want a chill summer.

After having heard this response over a thousand times, I don't need to ask what it means, but I always do. I tend to hear a variation on the same theme time and time again. *I want downtime.*

I don't want any chores.

I want to sleep as late as I can.

I don't want a curfew.

I want unlimited screen time.

I don't want to have any responsibilities.

I just want to hang out.

I don't want anything required of me.

On the one hand, I understand the desires. I'll be the first to champion a boy getting an opportunity to catch his breath. When I reflect on everything I know about how hard boys work to maintain focus and sit still throughout the school year, to bring their A game to their academic experience, I'm all for them having downtime and coming out from under that level of expectation and requirement.

What I also know to be true is that most boys aren't self-actualized enough to structure their time well. Left on their own they'd spend endless hours on technology, sleep until noon, stay up until the middle of the night, eat junk food, and avoid all chores and responsibilities. None of these habits would benefit them. In fact, we could easily argue less sleep, more screens, less responsibility, and more junk food would turn him into a monster. He'd be the worst version of himself.

As is the case with most things in life, it's about finding balance. How can we pull back the expectations of the academic year and make sure he still has responsibilities needed for whole development? How can we allow him to sleep in and not stay up until three in the morning? How can we enjoy a slower pace and still have structure?

Because he struggles to get there on his own, he'll need our input, oversight, and involvement. I'd certainly include his voice in the equation. Sit down prior to summer and talk about all the options—camps, vacations, work, chores, rest, exercise, technology, and goals. Help him set some goals for the summer. Go back to everything we discussed earlier in the book about making those measurable and manageable. Help him cast a vision for the things he wants and the places he needs to grow. Discuss family rhythms, expectations, and needs. Consider drafting a contract for the summer that spells out your expectations and his freedoms. Make it clear, concrete, and concise.

Map out a calendar where he can see the weeks he'll be out of town for different experiences and the weeks he'll be home. Boys benefit from having a visual to communicate the balance of all these things. As you seek work and volunteer opportunities, help him articulate his areas of passion and interest, and let that serve as a guide in your research for investing time well.

Most importantly, don't wait on him to show an overwhelming amount of interest or excitement in this process. Some boys will appreciate having this much ownership in the summer. I often hear boys say things like "My mom scheduled my entire summer away and I never had a say," or "I hate how much I was gone for the summer. I wish I'd been home more." Involving him in the planning can curb some of that negative input on the back side.

At the end of the day, the "structure" of this approach is likely to feel like requirement and expectation, and keep in mind what he wants in a "chill" summer. Tell him this kind of planning is training ground for him to know how to structure downtime and off time in his future as an adult. Although he can't fully make that connection now, it benefits him to hear it.

Often I hear parents say things like "He's not interested in mapping out the summer with me" or, "I keep bringing up talking about the summer and he keeps avoiding it." Often we're waiting on boys to get somewhere they can't get on their own. Keep going back to prioritizing his character over his happiness. It's the very reason we offer him the structure he can't know he needs.

The Healthy Mind Platter

The exact same process can be used with boys in thinking about the weeks or weekends. The long journey of developing structure and rhythms, habits and practices builds a life skill he will need and fall back on throughout development. When brainstorming with boys around these ideas, I encourage parents to use a tool called the Healthy Mind Platter. It was created by Dr. Daniel J. Siegel, executive director of the Mindsight Institute and clinical professor at the UCLA School of Medicine, in collaboration with Dr. David Rock, executive director of the NeuroLeadership Institute.

Think back to the food pyramid you studied in elementary school. It reminded us of the foods we should all include in our daily diet to optimize physical health. The Healthy Mind Platter has seven daily essential activities needed for optimizing mental health. The activities include focus time, playtime, connecting time, physical time, time in, downtime, and sleep time. These seven daily activities make up the "mental nutrients" your brain needs to function at its best.

There's an easy-to-find document online explaining the seven activities with ideas on how to integrate these into the every day, creating more balance.[1] Every family would benefit from printing off the list and talking together about the ways they experience and enjoy each of the seven activities, and which ones are harder and easier to fold in on a daily basis. The Healthy Mind Platter can be a great tool for developing goals as you work to achieve balance and fold in healthy habits and practices.

New Ways of Living

Physical, emotional, relational, and spiritual health don't just happen. We have to build habits and practices that support well-being. It's of great importance to build habits in all four areas. When I do goal-setting exercises with boys in my office, I always require them to create measurable and manageable goals in each category. During the school year, I'll have boys create academic and athletic goals, and during the summer the goals will be relevant to that season.

We discuss not only the importance of making goals measurable and manageable, but also how daily habits and practices move us toward the goals we want to accomplish. I remind boys that we are all capable of coming up with great ideas, but most people don't implement them. We don't *think* ourselves into new ways of living. We *live* ourselves into new ways of thinking.

Boys seem to attach to this logic because they are action-oriented creatures. They are great problem-solvers. They simply need support in putting those ideas into practice.

We talk about habits that no longer serve them—practices that haven't worked or sometimes haven't been practiced enough to work. I engage that problem-solving strength by helping them cross off old ideas and replace them with new ones. We talk about how habits and practices are body, mind, and soul strengthening disciplines. Talk with your son about these habits and practices as ways to live out the charge of Matthew 22:37, "Love the Lord your God with all your heart and with all your soul and with all your mind." We can't activate that calling until we have habits and practices in place.

On that note of practices that haven't been practiced enough, I've seen many boys get stuck in this place. Just this week I met with a twelve-year-old who has a long pattern of yelling at his parents and sister. When he's emotionally charged, he will periodically throw and break things. During his worst episode, he even pushed his mother. This incident prompted his parents to reach out for help. He'd been struggling for years, but it had never reached this point. His wise parents were understandably concerned about his entering into puberty and adding a biological tsunami, emotional intensity, and relational complexity to the mix.

As they were sharing observations, his parents tracked through a developmental history of colic, difficulties with sleep, sensory hurdles, and outbursts from the time he was a toddler. He'd seen an occupational therapist, feeding therapist, nutritionist, and school counselor. There was plenty of evidence on the table of where this young man had struggled navigating discomfort around food, textures, transitions, relationships, and emotions. He was easily triggered and went from zero to a hundred miles an hour in a matter of seconds.

We talked about setting the bar of expectation at a reasonable place. We discussed how repeating the same thought patterns and behaviors over time can create mental pathways our brains automatically take in the future. It's like traveling the same route home from work every day. It becomes so familiar we could almost do it in our sleep. This young man had been firing and wiring neurological pathways in navigating discomfort with outbursts for over a decade.

> **The architecture of our brain can change. We can always create new pathways.**

The good news is that the architecture of our brain can change. We can always create new pathways. It simply takes habits and practice. I reminded these parents that practice makes progress, not perfect. We aren't looking for night and day, or a complete 180. We are starting with a slow turning that includes a lot of practice.

The boy's mom added that a year ago he'd made a profession of faith and asked to be baptized. Following that event, he had a short period of reprieve, but then the outbursts started again. He'd "rededicated" his life to Christ three more times and once asked his mom if the pastor had put enough water on his head to "make baptism work." Do you see what was happening? He was 100 percent convinced that his profession of faith and baptism would turn around his behavior.

His parents had wonderful conversations with him, trying to walk him through some abstract concepts, in spite of his concrete thinking. They broke down what Scripture means when it talks about the battle between the spirit and the flesh.

They dissected Paul's words of doing what I don't want to do and not doing what I want to do.

They also wisely, wonderfully reminded their son that he played an important role in this equation. Yes, his decision meant the Spirit lived inside of him, but just as he had to make daily decisions to get enough sleep, eat nutritious foods, and exercise in order for his body to be healthy, he had to develop similar habits for his emotional health. His mom went a step further to talk about her grandfather, whom the boy had never known.

She told him that he went to church every week of his life and knew large amounts of Scripture, yet he also screamed at his family members and was abusive to her grandmother. She commented that he would have described himself as spiritually mature, and she would have described him as emotionally unhealthy. She went on to talk about the meaning of "These people honor me with their lips, but their hearts are far from me" (Matthew 15:8).

She used this as a jumping-off point for talking more about counseling and the whole family getting new ideas for how to navigate discomfort, whether it was plans changing unexpectedly, new foods at the dinner table, frustrations with a sibling, or time to turn off technology. She reminded her son they'd tried a lot of things together already, and none of it seemed to work well. It was time for some new ideas and a new "coach" in the mix.

Old Dog, New Tricks

Adding a new "coach" to the mix is ultimately asking for help—something we've discussed, and the research confirms, that is difficult for males. We have to train boys in that direction, as it simply isn't instinctive. We need to model this repeatedly for boys.

Many boys grow up hearing their moms talk about engaging friends, counselors, and spiritual directors. Few boys hear the men in their lives talk about doing this and all the layers of benefit in asking for help. We simply can't turn up the volume enough on this practice if we are going to turn the tide on the alarming statistics shared earlier in the book. Boys must see and hear evidence of men asking for help.

Equally so, they need to see men as students, embracing the idea that we always have more to learn. There is always room to grow. We simply don't know everything, and we need teachers, coaches, pastors, and guides throughout our lives. I once heard a pastor say, "I preach the gospel to myself every day because I forget it every day." He called this human reality "gospel amnesia." Despite the evidence of being adopted as sons and daughters of the King, we live, think, and act like orphans.

When boys see the men in their lives still learning, reading, growing, and desiring to change, they feel permission to need that for themselves. They stop believing there is an arrival date when they become a fully developed human here on earth, and they see heaven as the only arrival date, the point of completion.

In doing so, we also push against the adage that you can't teach an old dog new tricks. Just as the twelve-year-old had developed neurological pathways to patterns of volatility, he could develop new ones. We can develop new patterns as parents. It is possible to teach an old dog new tricks.

It's important to understand your particular triggers and

tendencies. For example, everyone who knows me knows that I have a sweet tooth. I think about sweets 24/7 (yes, even in my sleep). I crave them all the time. My wife is convinced I'm the only man who regularly eats "breakfast dessert." I can easily chase down eggs and bacon with cinnamon rolls, muffins, banana bread, and waffles.

Years ago I heard something on the news about leptin, the hormone that tells your mind to stop eating (signal of satiety). I am 100 percent convinced I have 0 percent of this hormone, because I never feel full and I'm always thinking about the next meal.

The news story proposed that by excluding processed foods, you could improve leptin sensitivity and thus induce better promotion of satiety hormones within your body. I decided to give it a try. By altering some things about my daily diet (at the recommendation of a cardiologist), I developed some new practices, including eliminating certain foods, not eating late at night, and trading in grazing experiences for walks around the neighborhood. In summary, I'm eating less and walking more. I'd love to report I'm craving less, but the truth of the matter is I could eat six cinnamon rolls right this minute.

Our *tendencies* may not change, but our *practices* can. I talk often about this with kids who struggle with anxiety. Understandably, all kids want it to go away and never come back. The reality is they may always struggle with anxiety to some degree, but they can develop skills and

> **Our tendencies may not change, but our practices can.**

strategies for living with it. I once did a family session with a single mom and her nine-year-old son. She had struggled with anxiety most of her life and began recognizing its presentation in her son early in his journey. She told her son how grateful she was for counseling and how much it had helped her. "If you happen to deal with anxiety for a long time like I have, I want you to be able to carry it with God." I loved the phrase *carry it with God*. The idea that her son could develop skills and strategies that would allow him to carry it throughout his life. And that he is never alone in it. He would always have God with him to walk through whatever anxiety he experiences.

The Four Categories

In thinking about developing habits and practices, it's good to start with general and specific work. Every person has both. We could define general work in terms of the four categories I mentioned earlier—physical, emotional, relational, and spiritual. An easy blueprint we could use for ourselves and the boys we love is this:

1. Identify the work
2. Set goals
3. Develop habits and practices

Let's start with **physical**. If the general work in this category was staying active in order to maintain health and longevity, I could set a goal of exercising three times a week. One habit could be to set a reminder in iCal (or your particular calendar app) on the days I have the most space to fit this in. Another habit could be to text a friend and plan a run. The ideas could be endless.

1. Stay active.
2. Exercise three times a week.
3. Set reminders in iCal.

Specific work in this category could include anything from a unique onetime goal like running a marathon or triathlon to recovering from a surgery or injury and engaging in physical therapy.

Let's take a look at some **spiritual** work. Theologian Tim Muldoon says,

> Ignatius wrote . . . spirituality is a practice, a regular endeavor through which we come to build our lives on the love of God—to order our lives according to God's plan for us. Its focus, then, is not primarily ourselves but, rather, God. In naming his spiritual practices "exercises," Ignatius sought to suggest something about how we approach them: as undertakings we must repeat again and again in order to progress slowly toward a goal. We can see spiritual exercises, then, as a part of regular maintenance for the soul. If we practice them, we will give ourselves the chance to know God more intimately and to know God's will for us.[2]

I'm drawn to the phrase *build our lives on the love of God*. If I'm devoted to building my life on the love of God, it speaks to the work and regular maintenance I want to be about. It's not work I have to do to earn God's love. That work is finished and complete. This is the work that deepens my understanding of his love and moves me more fully into intimacy with him.

Several habits I've formed over the years keep me aligned with this important work. I have a chair in my house where I begin every morning. I have a basket beside it with my Bible, my reading glasses (a sign of my age), and a candle I light every morning to usher in that time, and I enjoy a good cup of coffee. Having identified space and all of my belongings in one spot has made me more consistent in the time. I look forward to that first cup of coffee every morning, and something about anchoring it to these practices has enhanced my spiritual workout in the mornings.

1. Build my life on the love of God.

2. Read, pray, and journal daily.

3. Pour the first cup of coffee prior to the time.

Specific work in this area for a boy could include reading through the Bible in a year, studying a particular book, or perhaps joining the church and enrolling in a confirmation class.

For me, an example of **relational** work could be nurturing my marriage by time spent together. My wife and I both work outside the home and have been raising three kids who are actively involved in school and sports. I write and travel as part of my work, and if you combine all those ingredients, it makes alone time together a great challenge. We've learned the hard way, as many couples do, that time together doesn't happen without intention and planning. We have to schedule it in the way we have to schedule in trips to the grocery store, exercise, and daily chores. That may sound a bit mechanical to you, but it simply won't happen with consistency unless it's mapped out.

We live in a small house with three teenagers, and having private conversations can be a bit of a challenge. When our kids were little, I'd pick up late dinner once we got everyone to bed and we'd picnic in our living room. We hired babysitters when the budget allowed and got creative in different seasons. Once they were old enough to stay home alone, we'd go out for dinner without the cost of a sitter or do Saturday morning coffee runs.

Because we both want to stay active and healthy, we often hike in our local parks, or if we're crunched for time, we will simply walk in our neighborhood. We take hour-long walks and get the benefit of time together while squeezing in some exercise.

1. Nurture my marriage.
2. Take time alone together for at least an hour once a week.
3. Walk in the neighborhood every Sunday afternoon.

Many boys I work with are pretty disciplined and passionate about the physical work, although technology has hijacked a great amount of interest and investment in this area in the last decades. Boys who come from families with a strong faith commonly have some habits for developing their spiritual muscles. By adolescence, the motivation often lessens and is part of why boys need a community of like-hearted guys to maintain momentum—youth group, D-Group, Young Life, or some kind of campus ministry.

Boys are likely to be less engaged, invested, and intentional with their relational and emotional lives than girls. They tend to prioritize these the least, if at all. There's a great chance we'll need to labor longer in these categories to help them build the weaker social and emotional muscles.

Let's work with the classic suppression (or eruption) versus expression issue. Let the work fall under the umbrella of working through **emotions**. The goal could be less shutting down or blowing up. The habits could include journaling, taking walks to talk through frustrations, using the Space, or hanging the Top Five List in an easily accessible place.

1. Work through emotions.
2. Stop yelling or throwing objects when frustrated.
3. Go to the Space for a minimum of five minutes when emotionally charged.

The specific work might have to do with a boy's pattern of arguing with his mom when the timer goes off to signal gaming time is over.

Notice a theme of the work being more big picture. The goal being measurable and manageable. And the habits being daily or weekly steps toward the goal that's connected to the larger work. It's always about breaking things down into concrete steps for the boys we love. Boys get trapped in ideas and struggle with the execution of those ideas. Using a grid like this can help boys develop the skills of goal setting, alongside developing healthy habits and practices.

Individual Practices

Let's look at other examples of habits and practices for boys ranging from toddlers to teenagers as we think about developing within the four categories.

I'm working with an elementary-aged boy who is trying to run one mile every day for ninety days. He created a small incentive with his parents at the thirty-day mark, a slightly bigger one at the sixty-day mark, and a trip to a water park with his dad if he hits the ninety-day mark. He's currently on day sixty-two, and I'm cheering him on. He can articulate all of what running is accomplishing for him. He's acutely aware that it's helping him emotionally to have that daily release. He's wisely discovering that he has to target specific times of day to run or he simply won't get around to it.

He's folded the running goal into the spiritual category by walking for ten minutes after the mile and praying as he walks. I have enjoyed hearing him talk about the conversations he shares with God during the "cool down" part of his run. He calls it cool down conversations with God.

I work with a ninth grader who is new to the football team and aware that he's the low man on the totem pole when it comes to playing time. He's set a personal goal to practice strength and conditioning four days a week in hopes of getting noticed by the offensive coordinator. He, too, is aware of how much more regulated he is emotionally when he's training with consistency. It has become a context for him to understand more about the physicality of his emotions.

A middle-school boy I know tried to kill two birds with one stone by riding on his mom's stationary bike while doing his summer reading for thirty minutes a day. He loves outdoor biking as well, but he does half of his riding indoors to knock out a school requirement he doesn't enjoy as much. He finds reading easier to accomplish when his legs are moving.

An elementary-aged boy who has a habit of interrupting set a relational goal of always letting his sister report on her day first at the dinner table to practice listening before speaking. A high school boy set a relational goal of letting his sister choose the music on the ride to school, where he'd once had a "my car, my music" rule in place, which he came to understand was selfish.

A middle-school boy set an emotional goal of creating a visual cue with his parents when he gets argumentative and steps into a trap that typically earns him reductions in screen time. When his mom or dad touches their lips, it's his reminder that he's turning a conversation into an argument, and he goes straight to his room to check his Top Five List.

A toddler whose parents I see is keeping a feelings chart on the dining room table, and every family member passes the chart around at dinner and picks the two they felt the most that day.

Another toddler has a single mom who folded in a daily practice called "the morning huddle." She's working to help her son and daughter learn to identify the difference between wants and needs. Every morning after breakfast, the three of them sit in a circle and talk about the day. They begin the time with a feelings check-in using the feelings chart. Then each member identifies one thing they want and one thing they need. A need could be time alone in their room or one-on-one time with Mom. A want could be building a fort, making homemade Popsicles, going to the zoo, or staying up fifteen minutes past the usual bedtime.

A teenage boy I work with just got access to social media. He had to sign a contract outlining the terms of responsible use. His parents voiced concern about how quick he is to blurt out what he's thinking at home and give unsolicited advice to others. They required him to memorize 1 Thessalonians 4:11, which challenges us to "make it your ambition to lead a quiet life . . . [and] mind your own business," as a way of anchoring him to the reminder that it's not his job to correct people's opinions online or comment on anything he disagrees with. They are using this Scripture to train him that social media is the worst platform for disagreeing with others because of the lack of proximity and relationship.

A nine-year-old is working on sleeping alone through the night in his own bed. He has a tendency to stretch out the bedtime routine, ask for six cups of water, and then wander into his parents' room every time he can't fall asleep easily. His practices are progressive muscle relaxation and the counting game as he learns to settle his mind and body at night.

A five-year-old boy, whom his parents describe as the world's pickiest eater, is learning to navigate discomfort at mealtime through habitual exposure to new foods and engaging in dinner conversation with his family.

A highly competitive eleven-year-old is working on enjoying playing sports with friends and remembering it's a game and not the Super Bowl. He practices taking deep breaths and walking around the field when he feels sirens and alarms going off inside him that might otherwise end in an explosion.

An eight-year-old is working on reciprocity in relationship. His parents have given him feedback that he interrupts often, talks over others in conversation, and has difficulty letting his friends choose the game or activity they enjoy. The work is thinking of others more than himself, and the practice involves asking questions more than making suggestions.

Family Practices

Just as we are developing habits and practices and our kids are doing the same, consider folding in some daily, weekly, monthly, quarterly, and annual practices as a family.

I work with a family that prays daily for the person seated to their left at the breakfast table. If their dad is traveling for work, he tries to FaceTime in to maintain this daily habit with his wife and children.

I work with another family who check in at dinner each night with highs and lows from the day and feelings about the events that took place.

A family with adolescents chooses one weekend meal where everyone is home and cooks together. A short family meeting follows to talk about upcoming events, but it's also a check-in point for the entire family with active, busy schedules.

Two different divorced families I consult with have a regularly scheduled homemade pizza night followed by movies and conversation. They are wisely using films as opportunities to develop critical thinking.

A single mom I know with young children lets each kid have a "sleepover" in her room once a month. They pick the weekend night, and this habit has been something each kid counts down to every month.

Multiple families I see have a tech-free Sunday once a month, when no one in the family engages a screen for twenty-four hours. This practice is designed to promote conversation, connection, rest, and refueling.

Several families I've worked with over the years have a habit of one-on-one time with each kid once a quarter. It may be an all-day event or an overnight. Often they don't leave the city but might stay at a local hotel and enjoy the pool, order pizza, and watch movies in the room. This habit allows the parents to have focused individual time, which can be hard to get with multiple kids.

Four families with toddlers join up once a quarter to deliver food to families in need. They box food together at a local food drive and then caravan together to homes in the city, allowing their kids to have early exposure to meeting needs within their own city.

Many families I know plan an annual trip with extended family and create scavenger hunts with the cousins. This habit has continued well into the kids' college years, and they still look forward to this tradition.

An intentional family I work with gives each of their kids one hundred dollars for Christmas to donate to a nonprofit of their choice. The requirement is that they take the gift in person and connect with the organization through volunteering or education of some kind. They want the experience to involve connection and meaning.

Another family participates in a local mission trip each year. They don't leave the city limits but simply volunteer as a family in some capacity in hopes the practice reminds their kids of needs that exist all around them.

As we've discussed throughout this book, kids learn more from observation than information. Boys are experiential learners, and they make their best connections by going through the motions. These habits and practices set the groundwork not only for physical, emotional, relational, and spiritual growth, but also for making meaningful connections and developing valuable life skills.

Consider the different ideas throughout this chapter for building individual and family practices. Think uniquely about who your son is and where he most needs to grow. Think uniquely about the rhythms within your family. Where could you fold in new daily, weekly, monthly, quarterly, or annual practices? Possibly one of the ideas in this chapter or perhaps a new idea based on your understanding of who he is and what he needs.

Keep falling back on the wisdom of talking less about what you want for him and opening the door of opportunity for him to develop in that space experientially.

INTENTIONAL PRACTICES

1. **Evaluate summer.** Use summer as a framework for helping him develop skills around time management—brainstorming goals, planning downtime, goal setting, and forming habits and practices.

2. **The Healthy Mind Platter.** Download this valuable tool. Define the seven "nutrients" and brainstorm concrete ideas for each.

3. **Frame the four categories.** Help boys build a framework around physical, emotional, relational, and spiritual health. Identifying work, setting goals, and forming habits in these four areas will benefit him for life.

4. **Evaluate the four categories.** Set a time in iCal to review the work, goals, and habits, much like a performance evaluation. Explain this practice as something he will likely do throughout his vocational life.

5. **Read Matthew 7:24–27.** Talk about this parable and how the work, goals, and habits equation is connected to building on a solid foundation.

Conclusion

Moving Forward

I attended a high school football game years ago with my sons. We were taking in the smells of a crisp fall Friday night, the booming roar as the players ran onto the field for the first time, and the sounds of a community coming together to cheer on a team they love.

We weren't far into the first quarter when I encountered a mom seated on the bleacher behind us. She was small in stature, decked from head to toe in purple and gold, proudly wearing a pin-on button with her son's face, one of the star players. She was sandwiched between her younger children and her mother, who delightfully introduced herself as "the proud grandmother."

This mom was, shall we say, a vocal fan . . . celebrating yards gained, interceptions, and even failed attempts that held evidence of passion and heart. What struck me most about this dear woman was her enthusiasm for *every* young man on the field, not just her own son. He was a standout

173

receiver, but she could have been the mother of every boy who stepped onto the field. She knew their names and celebrated their plays as if they were her own flesh and blood.

She kept yelling, " I see you! Number fifty-two, I see you!" She would exchange their jersey number for their name: "Thomas, I see you."

This continued throughout the game, beyond halftime, and well into the fourth quarter when one of our players was injured. The team took a knee as the coaches and a team physician ran onto the field to assess the young man's injury. As they carried the boy off the field with tears rolling down his face, she stood and yelled, "I see you, John Mark. I see you, son." She stood and kept repeating the words again and again.

There was something so beautiful, so honoring about this woman's declaration. Three simple words—*I see you.* I kept thinking that night about how God speaks those words over us—*I see you.* He takes delight in seeing us, knowing us, and calling us by name. He sees us in our victories, in our attempts, and when we are limping off the field wounded and feeling defeated.

"*I see you.*"

Being seen and known is something every one of us craves. It's the human condition. To be seen when we're hurting or struggling is an act of love. When children are in distress or discomfort, we want to eliminate the pain. If we can see them and be present with them in the distress, there's an immediate shift in their physiological state.

We have to move *to* the emotion before we can help our kids move *through* the emotion. When we move toward our kids in moments of struggle, we are modeling empathy, helping them regulate their nervous system, and expanding their capacity for emotional flexibility.

Discomfort is the cost of being human. It's inescapable. It's something boys work hard to avoid, suppress, or numb. In doing so, boys believe they are demonstrating strength. When in reality, they are simply creating more fragility. The less a boy understands his emotional landscape the more fragile he becomes. Fragile and fractured. More segmented and less integrated.

In 2019, the American Psychological Association (APA) released its first ever guidelines for working with men and boys. The APA would "draw on more than 40 years of research showing that traditional masculinity is psychologically harmful and that socializing boys to suppress their emotions causes damage that echoes both inwardly and outwardly." The findings went on to say, "Masculine reluctance toward self-care extends to psychological help. Research led by Omar Yousaf, PhD, found that men who bought into traditional notions of masculinity were more negative about seeking mental health services than those with more flexible gender attitudes."[1]

Men's alignment with traditional masculinity, reluctance toward self-care and seeking help, and pushing aside difficult realities is why emotions have become gendered over time. This is also why emotional literacy is often defined as a soft skill—skills that are foundational to well-being, and yet we refer to them as "soft skills."

My great hope is inviting parents, educators, coaches, and anyone who loves boys into a new way of being.

A path that teaches boys suppression is maladaptive and unhealthy.

A path that teaches shutting down and blowing up are harmful, not helpful.

A path that confirms internal pain always has an external presentation.

A path that helps boys connect their head and their heart.

A path where toughness and tenderness coexist.

A path where empathy and awareness are seen as superpowers.

A New Way of Being

Mister Rogers is credited as saying, "If it's mentionable, it's manageable."[2] Fred Rogers lived the wisdom of those words, believing all children needed to be seen and known, and that having caring adults who could offer that would change everything. I remain grateful his voice is being elevated at this time in the world, many years after his death. I hope we continue to lean into the wisdom he offered us about understanding children and understanding ourselves. Mister Rogers once commented, "I don't think that the basics that kids need have changed in 10,000 years."[3] I'd add to that wisdom: I believe their needs will be the same ten thousand years from now. The question is how will we be attending to those needs and what will we be prioritizing?

For years I led a group of high school guys on Thursday nights. Each week we'd come together, sit around a big table, and eat burritos and queso. It's amazing how easily adolescent boys will talk about anything when queso is in the mix. My office is located down the street from a beloved burrito place that's locally owned and has incredible food. We'd grab food at the beginning and then situate ourselves around the table to talk about life—the things they were facing, the challenges of being an adolescent guy at this time in the world, and the hopes and fears they had for their futures. We'd spend time talking about how the world defines masculinity and what it could mean to broaden that definition. We discussed how the world defined strength and the way Christ defined it.

In the safety of that room, we celebrated graduations from high school and acceptances to colleges. We'd applaud a guy who got his driver's license and one who was working through the fear of asking a girl to prom. We celebrated first jobs, starting positions on a team, leads in the school play, summer internships, and scholarships. We grieved the loss of a parent, parents' marriage, friends, grandparents, and pets, and we grieved with a boy who lost his brother. We wept together over breakups, heartbreak, loss of dreams, and a member of the group being diagnosed with a chronic illness. In leading that group for over a decade, there wasn't a circumstance an adolescent boy could face that we didn't experience.

As old members of the group graduated from high school and moved forward, new members came into the group and the dynamic would change. The one thing that stayed the same was the guarantee of hearing every young man who joined the group at some point say a version of the same thing: "*I had no idea guys talked like this.*"

It's important to note here that I wasn't creating magic in the room. I don't have a skill set that can't be duplicated in any city on any given Thursday night. It was simply a safe place. There was no posturing required. The only requirement was to show up, and the expectations for the time were simple.

Show up.

Be honest.

No posturing.

No sarcasm.

Agree to disagree.

Respect each other.

I was sometimes asked if it was difficult to maintain those expectations, and I can honestly say it never was. It had very little to do with me and everything to do with them. I never had to enforce those expectations, because they required it of each other. They set the tone for the time, and any new member who wanted to try posturing or sarcasm discovered there was no place for it in the room. No one would tolerate it because no one was interested in it.

These guys lived in a posturing culture every day in their academic, athletic, and extracurricular lives. They all agreed it was exhausting to maintain, and the relief they'd experience when they could step out of that at home, in safe friendships, and in this room on Thursday nights was like being offered cold water on a hot day.

The queso and the burritos certainly got them in the room. But the safety and the freedom were what kept them there.

Every time I talked with a young man over the years about joining the group, it was met with anything from hesitation to resistance. My "pitch" included just sitting in and observing. I'd challenge them to be open to a different way of being with guys their age. Because most of them had never or rarely experienced it, I'm convinced they thought I was pulling something over on them. No one ever outwardly rolled their eyes at me, but I'm certain it happened internally.

I wouldn't blame them. If you'd tried to pitch me an honest conversation with guys my age when I was seventeen, I wouldn't have believed you either. Mostly because I didn't really think it existed. We don't know what we don't know. It's difficult to imagine what we haven't seen.

They were all craving something they didn't even know they needed.

Because guys almost never share with other guys how they are struggling and what they are needing, they carry those things alone. As desperate as we are to know we're not alone, many boys live that way.

Every time I sit with a boy whose parents are divorcing, I'll ask, "Do any of your friends know this is happening?" I can't tell you how often boys look at me with eyes that say, *Why in the world would I tell them that?* or *How would that possibly help?* It's as if it never occurred to them to reach out.

It's familiar to hold it in. It's foreign to reach out.

Part of why every boy, at some point, declares, "I had no idea guys talked like this" is because they've never seen it. They haven't tasted the satisfaction of being seen and understood by their peers. They may have experienced it with their dad. However, if their own dads never experienced it themselves, it's difficult for them to offer it to their sons. We can't give what we haven't received. We can only take our kids as far as we've gone ourselves.

The River and the Ripple

There's a famous saying that "there comes a point where we need to stop just pulling people out of the river. We need to go upstream and find out why they're falling in."[4] This book is all about heading upstream to find out where boys are falling in. I hope to interrupt a boy's current way of being in the world in a way that creates a ripple effect on his peers, his future spouse, and someday his own children. The statistics I shared in the beginning of this book are hard evidence of how we keep pulling males out of the river. Let's be done with devoting all our energy to rescue missions and let's do everything we can to become strategists.

Let's devote ourselves, as adults who care about boys, to becoming preventionists and not just interventionists.

If you're a parent or grandparent, tell boys you are learning right along beside them. You are committed to developing a more expansive emotional vocabulary. You plan to become more skilled in talking about the things you feel and not just what you do. You plan to become well versed in recognizing the signs your body is giving you when emotions register internally. As one seven-year-old told me, "I'm becoming an emotional ninja!" He went on to report how good he was getting at naming his feelings and figuring out what to do with them.

> **Let's devote ourselves, as adults who care about boys, to becoming preventionists.**

Let's have our Top Five List posted somewhere visible. Talk openly about what's working. Let boys see you heading to the Space. Create a travel Space that you can take to other places with stress balls, balloons to blow into, a journal, or any other objects that would be helpful.

If you're an educator, check out the great work Dr. Marc Brackett is doing at the Yale Center for Emotional Intelligence. Explore what it would mean to implement the RULER approach in your classroom. RULER stands for recognition, understanding, labeling, expression, and regulation.

Dr. Brackett describes RULER as "an evidence-based approach to social and emotional learning (SEL) . . . [that] supports entire school communities in understanding the value of emotions, building the skills of emotional intelligence, and creating and maintaining a positive school climate."[5] I dream of a day when every school is prioritizing social and emotional learning as much as (or more than) we prioritize math, reading, science, and social studies. For as long as we consider SEL skills to be soft skills or secondary learning, kids are missing out on a vital part of what they need to be great humans in this world.

Similarly, consider setting aside a corner of your classroom where kids can go to regulate. Some teachers call it the Calm Corner or the Peace Place and fill it with stress balls, fidget toys, a medicine ball, art supplies, or any activities that would support kids needing an outlet. Use a timer or an hourglass with sand to help kids make room for their peers to use the Space as well.

If you're a coach, I'd urge you to explore the great work my friend Scott Hearon is doing at the Nashville Coaching Coalition. NCC has a mission to "develop full-hearted coaches who prepare young people for life." They "envision a world where athletics teaches every kid that they belong and matter for who they are, not how they perform." This amazing organization is committed to equipping coaches to be transformational leaders through conferences, forums, trainings, and virtual groups. Scott and his team "believe youth athletics provides the most strategic opportunity to help young people be mentally and emotionally prepared for life."[6]

Consider using some part of your training time to watch movies like *My All American*; *Radio*; *The Blind Side*; *When the Game Stands Tall*; *Remember the Titans*; *Invincible*; *Facing the Giants*; *We Are Marshall*; *Rudy*; *Glory Road*; *Hoosiers*; *Hurricane Season*; *Coach Carter*; *Invictus*; *Bend It Like Beckham*; *Miracle*; *Eddie the Eagle*; *The Miracle Season*; *Soul Surfer*; *McFarland, USA*; *Chariots of Fire*; *Million Dollar Arm*; *American Underdog*; *The Rookie*; and *42*. Use films like these as team building exercises and opportunities to help players develop emotionally and teams build meaningful connections.

If you're a children's pastor, youth pastor, small group leader, Scout master, or camp counselor, I'd encourage you to think about all the ways you could fold social and emotional learning into the work you're already doing. Don't reinvent the wheel, and don't hear me assigning you a new curriculum or additional work. I simply want you to look for opportunities to help boys talk more about how they *feel* about the things they *do*. Consider downloading a feelings chart and having it at the ready as a staple to your time. Let it serve as a prompt for you to use more emotional vocabulary in your own day to day. Talk about the difference between suppression and expression. Consider taking an emotional agility quiz based on the outstanding research done by Dr. Susan David, a Harvard Medical School psychologist. You will immediately receive a free online report and a set of two-minute videos explaining emotional agility—what it means and how to develop more of it. The content will instinctively guide you in your interactions with boys in your work.[7]

Consider sharing more of your own experience (in an age-appropriate way) with struggle and fear and the constructive ways you are learning to work through stress and discomfort. Explain to boys how "diet" is really all that we take in on a daily basis, not just food. Our consumption of media, relationships, and spiritual content (or lack thereof) affects how we see the world and our way of being in the world. Share practices and habits you are finding to be helpful in your own journey. Not only do boys need to hear these stories, but they need to see adults they trust experiencing the full range of an emotional experience. Social media is tricking them into thinking life is a series of ideal moments and therefore something must be terribly wrong with their own life. We know social media is a highlight reel of carefully curated, highly edited moments that simply don't represent the full picture.

Helping boys find their way to the full experience of being human and being fully masculine is what we are chasing. Camping out in the stories and places of struggle not only gives them permission to have those but also teaches them skills for how to navigate them. They feel prepared to hit bumps in the road when they encounter them because they know they are coming and the adults they trust faced them as well. They not only faced them, but they shared their experience of how they moved through them.

This also sets the stage for modeling a life of faith in front of boys. It is hard evidence of how to move upward and outward. Share what it means to need God and community. What it looks like to open up, reach out, and ask for help.

The kind of help we all need. The kind of help we were designed not just to need, but to offer. It's anchoring them back to purpose and what they were made for in this world.

On that note, let's stop asking boys, "What do you want to do?" Let's start asking them, "Who do you want to be?"

Boys will instinctively tether themselves to their performance as students and athletes. They will feel the pull as adults to anchor their identity to vocation. Asking boys, "What do you want to do?" or men, "What do you do?" assumes this somehow defines our purpose and place in this world.

Let's land more in the space of "Who do you want to be?" That question also assumes we are all still on a journey to becoming that person, and we are. We are all students whether we're enrolled in school or not. The opportunities to learn and grow are all around us.

Yes, this is moving in a different direction.

Yes, it's swimming upstream.

Yes, it's hard work.

But I believe it's hard work that yields good growth.

Let's do the work together.

Acknowledgments

I have long believed my greatest strength is surrounding myself with people who outpace and upstage me. As long as I stay in close proximity to the folks named here, I can continue to convince others I know more than I actually do.

Thank you to the amazing team at Bethany House and Baker Publishing Group for all the ways you made this book a reality. In particular to Hannah Ahlfield for carefully reading through my first attempt at this content and helping shape it into what you hold today. This book would still be an idea in my head if it weren't for Jeff Braun, who championed this project from day one and believed I had something to say. Thank you for all the ways you've stood in support of me and this project.

The team at Minno, who make our podcast possible and share the mission of caring for kids and families. Jess and Denise, it's an honor to partner with you.

Jana Muntsinger is my favorite publicist on the planet and also a dear friend. I have always trusted your steady guidance and wisdom.

Carter Crenshaw, Trace Blankenship, John Allen, Dave Hunt, and Jerry Cargile have been pacesetters in my life for decades, and I have no interest in running this race without you in front of me. I have learned so much about what it means to be a husband, father, friend, and follower of Christ from watching each of you.

The staff at Daystar are some of the most talented, invested, generous folks I've had the privilege of knowing. I can't believe I get to go to work with people like you. So many of the stories in this book were birthed out of the amazing families I've encountered in twenty-five years of being at this incredible place. David, Sherman, Don, Tommy, Aaron, and Kenneth, thank you for raising emotionally strong boys every day in your work. Melissa Trevathan, thank you for inviting me to be a part of something so life-giving and meaningful.

Sissy Goff, I'm humbled by your words at the beginning of this book, and you really are my second sister. Every time we speak or record, I am learning something from hearing you, and I'm better for having been in your company.

Sharon, though I was your big brother, you have always been ahead of me. As I talk about the stages of development, you lived through every one of those with much grace and patience. Jim, I'm thankful you joined our family, and you quickly became the MVP.

Bob and Amy, I don't consider you in-laws but siblings. I'm grateful to call you and your children my family. Peggy, you and Robert welcomed me from day one and handed over your greatest asset. I will always be indebted to you.

Dad, there's a reason I asked you to be the best man in my wedding. You are the best man I know in this world. Losing your wife, my dear mom, has been the greatest loss of my life. Having you move close to us after that loss has been one of the greatest joys. I am still learning from you, and I am certain I always will.

Connie, someone should place an Olympic gold medal around your neck for carrying me across the finish line of this manuscript. As in all of life, you have cheered and celebrated, challenged and championed, listened and labored with me. As I have long told our children, "Marrying your mother is the best thing I ever did for you."

Lily, Baker, and Witt, I'm pretty certain my job was to raise the three of you, but I think you've ended up raising me. I love having a front row seat to who you are becoming. I hope I end up like the three of you when I grow up.

Notes

Chapter 1: Traps and Tricks

1. Jane Wharton, "Heartwarming Moment Brother Helps Sister Play Basketball Then Tells Her 'You're Strong'," *Metro*, October 16, 2018, https://metro.co.uk/2018/10/16/heartwarming-moment-brother-helps -sister-play-basketball-then-tells-her-youre-strong-8041202.

Chapter 3: Backward and Forward

1. "Study of 800-Million Tweets Finds Distinct Daily Cycles in Our Thinking Patterns," University of Bristol press release, June 20, 2018, https://www.bristol.ac.uk/news/2018/june/twitter-study.html.

Chapter 4: Anxiety and Depression

1. Jamie Millar, "Meet the Man Bear-Crawling a Marathon," *Men's Health*, March 8, 2020, https://www.menshealth.com/uk/fitness/a33443922 /devon-levesque-bear-crawl-marathon/.

2. Benita N. Chatmon, "Males and Mental Health Stigma," American Journal of Men's Health 14, no. 4 (July 2020), https://journals.sagepub .com/doi/10.1177/1557988320949322.

3. "About Us," Movember, https://us.movember.com/about/mental -health.

4. "Our Impact Investment Strategy," The Movember Foundation, https://us.movember.com/uploads/files/Our%20Work/OurImpact_In vestmentStrategy.pdf.

Chapter 5: Moms and Dads

1. Gina Bria, *The Art of Family* (IUniverse: Bloomington, IN, 2011).

Chapter 8: Upward and Outward

1. Susan David, *Emotional Agility* (New York: Penguin, 2018), 39–40, 86.

2. Tara Parker-Pope, "The Science of Helping Out," *The New York Times*, April 9, 2020, https://www.nytimes.com/2020/04/09/well/mind/coronavirus-resilience-psychology-anxiety-stress-volunteering.html.

3. P. S. Mueller, D. J. Plevak, and T. A. Rummans, "Religious Involvement, Spirituality, and Medicine: Implications for Clinical Practice," *Mayo Clinic Proceedings* 76, no. 12 (December 2001): 1125.

4. Jim Robbins, "Ecopsychology: How Immersion in Nature Benefits Your Health," *Yale Environment 360*, January 9, 2020, https://e360.yale.edu/features/ecopsychology-how-immersion-in-nature-benefits-your-health.

5. Katherine and Jay Wolf, *Suffer Strong* (Grand Rapids, MI: Zondervan, 2020), 215.

6. Frederick Buechner, *Wishful Thinking: A Theological ABC* (New York: Harper & Row, 1973), 95.

7. Richard Rohr, *Things Hidden* (Cincinnati: Franciscan Media, 2008), 25.

Chapter 9: Habits and Practices

1. You can find a helpful visual of the Healthy Mind Platter at https://www.ledarskaphalsa.se/wp-content/uploads/2017/12/mindplatter.png.

2. Tim Muldoon, *The Ignatian Workout* (Chicago: Loyola Press, 2004), xiv.

Conclusion

1. Stephanie Pappas, "APA Issues First-Ever Guidelines for Practice with Men and Boys," *American Psychological Association* 50, no. 1 (2019), https://www.apa.org/monitor/2019/01/ce-corner.

2. Fred Rogers, quoted by Rick Fernandes, "Anything Mentionable," Fred Rogers Center, February 13, 2018, https://www.fredrogerscenter.org/2018/02/anything-mentionable/.

3. Fred Rogers, quoted by Eileen Ogintz, "Neighborhood Hero," *Chicago Tribune*, March 6, 1988, https://www.chicagotribune.com/news/ct-xpm-1988-03-06-8804050228-story.html.

4. This quote is often attributed to Desmond Tutu.

5. Marc Brackett, "*RULER*," https://www.marcbrackett.com/ruler/. See also https://www.rulerapproach.org/.

6. Nashville Coaching Coalition, https://nashvillecoachingcoalition.com/about-us.

7. Susan David, "The Quiz: Emotional Agility," https://www.susandavid.com/quiz.

About the Author

DAVID THOMAS, LMSW, is the director of family counseling at Daystar Counseling (daystarcounseling.com) in Nashville and the author or coauthor of ten books, including the bestselling *Wild Things: The Art of Nurturing Boys* and *Are My Kids on Track? The 12 Emotional, Social, and Spiritual Milestones Your Child Needs to Reach*. He is a frequent guest on national television shows and podcasts, and he co-hosts his own podcast called *Raising Boys and Girls*; he has been featured in publications like the *Washington Post* and *USA Today*; and he speaks across the country.

He and his wife, Connie, have a daughter, twin sons, and a yellow lab named Owen. You can follow David on social media at raisingboysandgirls and find the latest parenting resources at raisingboysandgirls.com.